CW01455332

JOHN ON JESUS AND ETERNAL LIFE

Mick Lockwood

DayOne

Endorsements

Whenever Mick Lockwood talks about Jesus I definitely want to listen. What you have here is a wonderful guide to Jesus Christ, exactly true to the facts—exciting, challenging and even shocking at times, and most definitely life-changing, if you take the challenge. Packed with stories to make you think (and sometimes laugh!), and, above all, full of the Bible's teaching, John on Jesus and Eternal Life is the perfect introduction to who Jesus is, what he came to do, and what he means for everyone. Highly recommended.

Dr Lewis Allen
Senior Pastor, Hope Church, Huddersfield

Now here is a book worth reading. Whether you have an active faith or not, this is important. With a keen eye for the truth, and a brilliant touch of storytelling, Mick Lockwood talks like a real person, explaining something both rare and essential for anyone living and thinking in our modern world today. He writes well, and so he should—he is showing us nothing less than the genuine promise of eternal life ... and how to get it. I told you it was important!

Norman Stone, Film Director

My friend Mick Lockwood is a Yorkshire man who is easy to talk to and easy to listen to. Even if you believe nothing at all, it is a sheer pleasure to sit with an open Bible and to hear him explain what it says and what it means; not everyone can have this pleasure. His brief book about the beginning of John's Gospel is the next best thing.

Stuart Olyott, Author and Retired Pastor

Published in Great Britain by
Day One, Ryelands Road, Leominster, HR6 8NZ
Email: sales@dayone.co.uk
Website: www.dayone.co.uk

British Library Cataloguing in Publication Data available

ISBN: 978-1-84625-804-6

Cover design by Kathryn Chedgzoy

Printed by 4edge

Contents

Introduction: The purpose of this book

I want to tell you what I have found. I found it in my early 20s when I wasn't looking for it. I didn't even know it existed but there it was. It was not hidden in some secret place, difficult to find, but totally accessible to anyone who desires it—even for someone like me who happened to stumble across it.

What I found was eternal life—not just living for ever with all the hardships of this life, but I found a life that will overcome the death of the body and, with a new body, enjoy a life without tears, death, sorrow, crying or pain.

I realize for many that will sound like a bad joke. Too incredible, even uncredible—literally without any credibility.

I was once preaching in the open air in St. Ives, Cornwall, when, to illustrate eternal life was real and free, I offered a ten-pound note to the first person who would take it from my hand; no conditions, no obligations, no questions asked—just take it. I had to put it back in my pocket because no one took up the offer. They couldn't believe there was no catch. I tried that illustration a few more times until someone took the note. Not being a rich man, I found another illustration to make the point, but the lesson still stands. If something seems too good to be true, as the saying goes, it usually is.

A quality eternal life! Does it exist? Could it ever be there for the taking, and free?

The early settlers in the west of the U.S.A. included many people who were eager to make money, and not all of them wanted to do so honestly. There were those who would concoct a 'Lily the Pink' medicinal compound which they claimed would be 'most efficacious in every case'—the cure-all remedy. Some were taken in and the fake medicine man got rich with his snake oil. But most would see it for what it was: a bad joke. So, here we have an introduction which talks about the gift of eternal life. Our experience of life tells us to tread carefully.

I remember how skeptical I was when I first heard this message:

> For God so loved the world that He gave His only begotten Son, that whoever believes in Him should not perish but have everlasting life (John 3:16).

But let me be more precise; what I actually found was a person—a person who gives eternal life: Jesus, God's only begotten Son, who is not known as dishonest or a joker, and is the exact opposite of a fake medicine man. This is what he said:

> I am the resurrection and the life. He who believes

> in Me, though he may die, he shall live. And whoever lives and believes in Me shall never die. Do you believe this? (John 11:25–26).

I am going to use the Bible, often referred to as 'Scripture', to introduce Jesus. The Gospels of Matthew, Mark and Luke, telling us of the life of Jesus, had already been written before the apostle John added his eyewitness account. John was as close as anyone to Jesus. Originally a fisherman, he had been convinced that Jesus was worth following. He witnessed everything firsthand, from his teaching, miracles, death and resurrection to his return to heaven. John tells us plainly why he wrote his Gospel: '... that you may believe that Jesus is the Christ, the Son of God, and that believing you may have life in His name' (John 20:31).

I have spoken to some people in the past who have thought the historical details of Jesus' life cannot be credible because they were written by his believing disciples and, therefore, must be biased and unreliable. That puts John in a difficult position, because he was a believer in Jesus as a result of hearing and seeing him as an eyewitness. It is a bit like seeing a great footballer but not being allowed to testify how great they are because you are now a fan.

It is worth remembering that being a follower of Jesus was a very dangerous business in the lifetime of the first disciples. The fake medicine man would hope to get rich. But the disciples of Jesus could not look forward to all this world has to offer; they would only see hardship, opposition and, for most of them, an early death through persecution. It is not a great incentive if they set out to collaborate in a pack of lies.

There are a number of excellent reasons why we can trust John's testimony of Jesus, but we will simply let him speak for himself and look at the opening passage of his Gospel, while referring to other parts of the Bible to shed light on its meaning. I am using the New King James version of the Bible, and when I quote other passages, the reference is noted in brackets, stating the Bible book it is from, followed by a number which is the chapter, followed by a colon and then another number referring to the particular verse. This book's aim is to show Jesus' and the Bible's teaching and gives you the opportunity to check out the verses in their context. It is also worth mentioning that the use of language is ever changing and, when the Bible was first written, it was common practice to address a group of male and female hearers using only the masculine gender but understood by all to include both male and female. You will come across this in some of the quotations to which I refer.

The Bible is a collection of sixty-six books. The first part of the Bible contains thirty-nine books which collectively are referred to as the Old Testament. These were all written before Jesus was born and were known by him. He used them as his foundation in all he had to say. The Old Testament is sometimes referred to as 'the law and the prophets' and Jesus tells us his own view of their reliability when he says:

> Do not think that I came to destroy the Law or the Prophets. I did not come to destroy but to fulfill. For assuredly, I say to you, till heaven and earth pass away, one jot or one tittle will by no means pass from the law till all is fulfilled (Matthew 5:17—18).

The twenty-seven books of the New Testament cover the period of Jesus' life and a few decades afterwards and were written by the apostles who had been chosen by Jesus or, in a few cases, their immediate associates.

As for me, when I learned more about Jesus, I became increasingly convinced I could trust this man and found faith in my heart to believe in him. I have never regretted it. I also discovered I had not accidentally stumbled upon him at all, but he had sought me out and found me. I write this book knowing God is continually seeking people out to show Jesus to them, so they too may know everlasting life:

> [He] is longsuffering toward us, not willing that any should perish but that all should come to repentance (2 Peter 3:9).

1 Who is Jesus?

The Gospel of John, chapter 1, verses 1 to 5 says:

In the beginning was the Word, and the Word
was with God, and the Word was God.
He was in the beginning with God.
All things were made through Him, and without
Him nothing was made that was made.
In Him was life, and the life was the light of men.
And the light shines in the darkness, and
the darkness did not comprehend it.

JESUS IS THE WORD.

John immediately introduces Jesus to us and enables us to plunge with him into the deep end of Scripture. He names a person, 'the Word'. We know he is talking about Jesus because the rest of the passage makes it clear and he goes on to say, 'the Word became flesh and dwelt among us, and we beheld His glory' (John 1:14).

Jesus is referred to in the Bible by many names, and 'the Word' is one of them. It conveys to us the idea of God expressing and communicating himself in the person of Jesus.

Other parts of the Bible make this clear.

In Colossians, Jesus is described as 'the image of the invisible God' (Colossians 1:15). On one occasion, Philip—one of his disciples—asked, '"Lord, show us the Father [referring to God], and it is sufficient for us." Jesus said to him, "He who has seen Me has seen the Father"' (John 14:8–9).

Bearing in mind God is invisible, Jesus was not saying he physically resembled God the Father, but he perfectly reflected all that is God. All Jesus' thoughts and words, his behaviour and work, his motives and desires are a mirror image of the Father, to enable us to see God.

That is why he is called 'the Word': 'No one has seen God at any time. The only begotten Son, who is in the bosom of the Father, He has declared Him' (John 1:18). God shows us himself in Jesus. We do not have to make guesses about God. He has made himself known. If we see Jesus, we see the Father.

We do not have to make guesses about God. He has made himself known. If we see Jesus, we see the Father.

JESUS IS GOD.

John takes us back as far as it is possible to go, before Creation and time itself. The first book in the Bible, Genesis, begins at the same point: 'In the beginning God created the heavens and the earth' (Genesis 1:1). John tells us that 'In the beginning was the Word, and the Word was with God' before the creation, and tells how that can be so: because 'the Word was God'.

In the account of Creation in Genesis, we read: 'Then

God said, "Let Us make man in Our image, according to Our likeness"' (Genesis 1:26). That verse in Genesis does not explain why God speaks of himself in the plural. It cannot be because there is more than one God. The Bible is very clear in teaching there is only one God, and the believing community of the Old Testament had as their watch cry: 'Hear, O Israel: The Lord our God, the Lord is one!' (Deuteronomy 6:4).

God, speaking about himself in the plural, does, however, prepare us for further revelation to come. There is only one God but, as the Bible unfolds, it teaches us the Father is God, the Son Jesus is God, and the Holy Spirit is God. This was Jesus' view of himself, and the religious leaders of the day clearly understood him and accused him of blasphemy because he was 'making Himself equal with God' (John 5:18). That was the prime reason they insisted on Jesus being crucified.

Yet, Thomas worshipped him as 'My Lord and My God!' when he saw him alive again after his crucifixion. Jesus did not say he was mistaken but accepted his worship saying, 'Thomas, because you have seen Me, you have believed. Blessed are those who have not seen and yet have believed' (John 20:28, 29).

JESUS IS THE CREATOR.

I wonder if you believe the world was created, or just came about by random chance? John had no doubt it had been created. However, his task here is not to try and convince us of that, but to tell us who created it. It was 'the Word', Jesus himself: 'All things were made through Him' (1:3). The Gospel of John, like the rest of the Bible, is written as a revelation from God, claiming to give us information which we cannot obtain through any other means. For this reason, it gives us statements about God and his characteristics: what he has said, what he has done, is doing and what he will do—and what he requires from us. One of the things it tells us is that he created the entire universe and everything in it.

The Bible also speaks directly to the ongoing debate as to whether there is a God or not and whether our universe has been created or come about by random chance. The apostle Paul tells us our observation of the universe is sufficient evidence in itself that the world must have been made and the God who made it must be eternally powerful. He goes on to say that these conclusions are not just for a few spiritual or religious people, but they can so clearly be seen by all; we have no excuse if we deny it.

Now this may appear unsatisfactory to some, as there are many people in the world who are simply not convinced that God even exists, let alone created everything, so how can it be claimed it is plain and clear to everyone? In the same passage of the Bible (Romans 1:18–22), the apostle Paul, who was personally chosen by Jesus, explains what the problem really is. When people say, as I once said myself and have heard many times from others, 'I don't think there is enough evidence to believe there is a God,' it fails to take into account the Bible's explanation as to why we say that.

Let us follow the Bible's reasoning. If it is true we were made by God, we are accountable to him and will be judged by him. Yet we are, says the apostle Paul, all capable of resisting God and suppressing truth because we are by nature in opposition to God. It is for this reason that we would rather take him out of our thinking altogether than face the reality of being answerable to him. We would rather put him in the dock than be there ourselves.

We would rather take God out of our thinking altogether than face the reality of being answerable to him.

'No,' says Paul, 'God's existence and his creation are plain and clear to see.' Our problem is our heart. I use the word, 'heart', here as the Bible often uses it, not referring to the physical organ that pumps blood through our body, but as the real inner you and me—the centre of all we are. We do not wish to see what is obvious because of all the consequences that it brings. We do not wish to be answerable to him. It is not an intellectual problem, but a problem of the human heart.

Yet John does not weigh up the pros and cons but simply declares Jesus as the Creator.

The apostle Paul goes one step further and tells us, 'All things were created through Him and for Him' (Colossians 1:16).

It is fashionable to take as a given that there is no meaning to life. The very thought of anyone suggesting in earnest a meaning to life is considered a joke in itself.

This was brought home to me some years ago when passing a park in Bradford, West Yorkshire. I saw what I thought to be a dozen priests playing leapfrog. Closer investigation revealed they were not priests at all but cardinals, crouching down in turn for the others to jump over them and enjoying an old children's pastime which, even then, children had long since abandoned.

It was of course a film set. After filming came to a pause, a man who was clearly an important member of the crew was standing by himself taking notes, so I took the opportunity to ask him what they were making. He explained it was the Monty Python comedy team making a film called, *The Meaning of Life*. As a Christian who actually believes there is a meaning to life, it was irresistible to ironically ask, 'Have you found it?' Knowing something of the very British satire they had produced in the past, I was expecting an ironic smile back. Instead, it was a pained grimace. 'It's a joke,' he retorted in all seriousness, before marching off in disgust.

I have always found incidents like this priceless. You receive a little first-hand insight into how people are thinking. It was a comedy film: a joke. But, for at least one important member of the crew, it was deadly serious; there is no meaning to life.

So, can we still ask the question, 'What is life all about?' Well, the comedy answer, 'You do the Hokey Cokey, and you turn around, that's what it's all about,' would seem as good an answer as any, if life is random with no meaning or plan. But if Jesus did make everything, as John claims, and everything was made for him, it would provide the foundation of beginning to understand the meaning and purpose of our lives.

Indeed, if it is true, we cannot make any sense of our world or our lives without knowing the central role of Jesus. I heard a helpful illustration a few years ago which likens looking at life without Jesus to watching a football match on an infra-red camera; these are the cameras which detect heat rather than light—the ones police helicopters use to see people and vehicles in the dark. The infra-red camera could pick up all the players because they transmit heat, but the cold ball at the centre of the action would remain unseen. You would see lots of

We cannot make any sense of our world or our lives without knowing the central role of Jesus.

players running around but for what purpose when you cannot see the ball?

So it is with trying to understand life without Jesus the Creator and the point of life itself. There is no real meaning to be found without him. But if we and all creation were made for him, we now know in which direction to look for more answers: towards Jesus.

JESUS IS THE SOURCE OF ALL LIFE.

We can see how John, the Gospel writer, is building brick by brick a picture of who is Jesus. He now tells us, 'In him was life' (1:4).

You and I have life because it has been given to us. Jesus has life in himself without having to rely on any outside source. Even when he faced death, he was able to say:

> I lay down My life that I may take it again. No one takes it from Me, but I lay it down of Myself. I have power to lay it down, and I have power to take it again (John 10:17b–18).

Jesus, then, did not see his death as an unavoidable consequence over which he had no power, but rather as a voluntary choice he himself had made. According to his own view, no one had the power to take life from him because he himself was the source of all life. Quite a claim! When we see Jesus' claims, we understand why it is impossible to think of him as simply a great teacher, because he does not leave us that option. As C. S. Lewis famously commented that, he must be either a liar, seriously deluded, or exactly who he says he is. Those three choices remain our only options.

What John is saying is that whatever life we are talking about, we can trace it back to Jesus, the source of all life—whether it is the life of every living creature and organism, or the spiritual life about which the Bible speaks. Jesus himself teaches we 'must be born again' (John 3:7), referring to the necessity of us receiving spiritual life through him.

It is this spiritual life John seems to have in mind when he now tells us, '... and the life was the light of men' (1:4). One of the things Jesus says is, 'I am the light of the world. He who follows Me shall not walk in darkness, but have the light of life' (John 8:12). John is pointing out that we are dependent on Jesus, the very source of life, for our life with God. Without him shedding light into our hearts and minds, we are incapable of knowing God at all. We remain in darkness, unable to see spiritually. This idea of receiving a life which brings light with it, is what the apostle Paul teaches when he writes to Christians saying, 'You were once darkness, but now you are light in the Lord. Walk as children of light' (Ephesians 5:8).

John, then, is presenting Jesus to us as the Word, God himself, the Creator who has life in himself, and as the light in whom we can see and know God. But, as he completes his description of who Jesus is, he leaves us with a sad footnote: 'The light shines in the darkness, and the darkness did not comprehend it' (1:5). Like a deep cavern receives not one shaft of light on the brightest and sunniest of days, so the impenetrable darkness of the human heart and mind remain untouched even after Jesus, the light of the world, has lived among us. Jesus, the source of all life, has eternal life to give but is the human heart ready to receive it?

Jesus, the source of all life, has eternal life to give but is the human heart ready to receive it?

2 What did Jesus come to do?

The Gospel of John, chapter 1, verses 6 to 9 says:

There was a man sent from God, whose name was John.
This man came for a witness, to bear witness of
the Light, that all through him might believe.
He was not that Light, but was sent to
bear witness of that Light.
That was the true Light which gives light to
every man coming into the world.

John, the Gospel writer, now turns to his namesake, John the Baptist—so called because he baptized those who accepted his message. We are told he was sent from God 'to bear witness of the Light' (1:7), the Light being Jesus. This is particularly made clear because the continued expectation was that one day, the Messiah would come and, as John the Baptist had such an impact on the whole region, some may have mistaken him for the expected Messiah.

'*Messiah*' is a Hebrew word, the language of the Old Testament, meaning 'the anointed one'. In Greek, the language the New Testament was written in, the word used with the same meaning is 'Christ'. The Old Testament carried with it this central theme that God would send his chosen King who would be their Saviour. As the old kings of Israel were anointed when they became king, in the same way the word, 'Christ', carried with it the hope of a great King to come.

John the Baptist also made it clear that he was not the Christ, but he had come to prepare the people for the appearance of the Christ. His task was the same as the Gospel writer's: to testify of Jesus 'that all through him might believe' (1:7). He was preaching in the desert when Jesus, now around the age of thirty, began his public ministry. His first task was to go and see John the Baptist, who had been telling the thousands of people that flocked to hear him from the surrounding towns and cities, to prepare for the Lord's arrival.

As John the Baptist's task was to bear witness to Jesus, what then did he have to say? The best summary is found a little further on in John's first chapter:

> The next day John saw Jesus coming toward him, and said, 'Behold! The Lamb of God who takes away the sin of the world!' (John 1:29).

John's Gospel began by telling us who Jesus is; John the Baptist now tells us what he came to do. Without any knowledge of the Old Testament, John's announcement concerning Jesus seems strange to us, but it is simple enough if we know the background. Let's take it step by step.

WHAT IS MEANT BY 'SIN'?

The Bible tells us God gave Moses Ten Commandments for the Israelites to follow. The first four are about our relationship with God and the other six are about our relationship with each other (Exodus 20:1–17). Here is a summary of those Commandments:

1. You shall have no other gods before Me.
2. You shall not make idols.
3. You shall not take the name of the LORD your God in vain.
4. Remember the Sabbath day, to keep it holy.
5. Honour your father and your mother.
6. You shall not murder.
7. You shall not commit adultery.
8. You shall not steal.
9. You shall not bear false witness against your neighbour.
10. You shall not covet.

In the same way as a car manufacturer would give instructions on how to operate your car, so God provided these instructions for how best the human being can function. Although these commands were originally given to the Israelites, they are all either directly quoted or further explained in the New Testament. Some laws given in the Old Testament were specifically for the Israelites and their situation, but these Ten Commandments remain the standard, right to the end of the Bible and to us. They tell us what God requires and mark out a boundary which we are told not to cross.

When John the Baptist, or Jesus, talks about sin, they are speaking of our transgressions—when we have crossed that boundary which God has set. This is what we are told not to do, and it is the constant definition of sin right through the Bible, as John explains elsewhere by saying, 'Whoever commits sin also commits lawlessness, and sin is lawlessness' (1 John 3:4). Sin is therefore defined as the transgressing of God's law.

There is, however, a positive application to these commands of what we are to do. When Jesus was asked, 'Which is the great commandment in the law?' he replied by saying:

> You shall love the LORD your God with all your heart, with all your soul, and with all your mind. This is the first and great commandment. And the second is like it: You shall love your neighbour as yourself. On these two commandments hang all the Law and the Prophets (Matthew 22:36–40).

Jesus summarized all the commandments God has given by simply saying, 'Love God and love your neighbour.' That basically is all God has ever asked of us: love. Is it a terrible requirement? Is it irksome? Can we say it is not fair? As every human being has the capacity to love, we can acknowledge how much sense that makes, when we recognize the love spoken of here is not solely based in our feelings but in respect to the creator God and all the people he has made. The commandments are given to direct that love. We do not want to be lied to, so we are not to lie to others; we do not want to be stolen from, so we are not to steal from others. Jesus sums it up by saying, 'Therefore, whatever you want men to do to you, do also to them, for this is the Law and the Prophets' (Matthew 7:12).

It is in one sense no surprise that God commands us to love as we are told in the Bible that 'He who does not love does not know God, for God is love' (1 John 4:8). The very essence of God is love.

It is for this reason sin is looked upon as a personal affront to God himself. David was the King of Israel 1,000 years before Jesus, and his prayer for forgiveness is a good example of this. He had committed adultery with a woman named Bathsheba and, when she became pregnant, David arranged for her husband Uriah to be killed so he could marry her. When he finally sees his guilt, he pleads with God for mercy and says:

> My sin is always before me. Against You, You only, have I sinned, and done this evil in Your sight' (Psalm 51:3–4).

David must have been aware that many people had been harmed by his actions, but what concerned him most was he knew the wickedness of what he had done was directed at God himself. That is why we must dig deeper to fully understand how seriously the Bible presents the subject of sin. Without understanding this we can make no progress in understanding why Jesus came and what he can do for us.

Remembering what we said before of how the Bible uses the word, 'heart', to describe the centre of our inner being, we have God's estimation of the real state of human beings given to us in the book of Jeremiah: 'The heart is deceitful above all things, and desperately wicked; who can know it?' (Jeremiah 17:9).

This was not the first time God had told us what the human heart is like. In the Bible book of Genesis, we read, 'The LORD saw that the wickedness of man was great in the earth, and that every intent of the thoughts of his heart was only evil continually' (Genesis 6:5). The apostle Paul in the New Testament says we are all under sin: 'There is none righteous, no, not one' (Romans 3:10).

One of the characteristics of God is that he is righteous. This means he is perfect in all his ways and without fault. We, however, are described as being deceitful and wicked right at the centre of our being. We are unrighteous, and it is this unrighteousness which separates us from God. We are told by the apostle Paul our hostility to God means we have placed ourselves as enemies of God and therefore, in that condition, cannot please him (Romans 8:7–8).

This does not mean every human being is incapable of doing good. We have the capacity to be kind, merciful, just and so on. But what it does mean is that sin is not just a wrong decision or act here and there, but it is the result of hearts that are corrupt. We are bad at our core, which means even at our best, our motives and attitudes carry with them the pollution of our heart.

Now for obvious reasons this is not a popular view. But I am presenting the world view of Jesus Christ and his diagnosis of the cause of the problems of the human being. The fact that something is radically wrong with the world we live in hardly needs to be spelled out as it is obvious to all. Our society, however, tends to assume people are basically good, but just a few 'monsters'– to quote the news outlets and social media sites—do wicked things. We may assume we are very different from these 'monsters', as we would never dream of doing the things they do.

Some years ago, I read a book called *A Human Being Died That Night*, by Professor Pumla Gobodo-Madikizela, a highly trained clinical psychologist. She spent many hours in conversation with the man who had been the commanding officer of the apartheid death squads at the height of South Africa's apartheid. He had been sentenced to 212 years for crimes against humanity and was nicknamed 'Prime evil'; a true 'monster' if ever there was one.

Pumla wanted to look into his heart to try and learn lessons of how he came to be a cold killing machine. When, with tears in his eyes, he told her, 'I wish I could do much more than say I'm sorry. I wish there was a way of bringing their bodies back alive,'[1] Pumla could no longer classify him as simply a 'monster' as now she was talking to a human being. She says in her book she realized something she was not prepared for: '... that good and evil exist in our lives, and that evil, like good, is always a possibility. And that was what frightened me.'[2]

In his preface to the book, Nelson Mandela wrote:

> The subtext is that if we fail to understand the nature and power of the forces that make for evil—forces that often lie just beneath the surface of most societies—they are likely to reoccur in one form or another at some time in the future.[3]

We can, to some extent, trace the causes of how inhumane regimes take control. Both Pumla, and Nelson Mandela can teach us much, but the Bible digs deeper still to reveal the true problem of this world. It is sin in the human heart.

We need not look at extreme examples to discover what the human heart is really like. I once witnessed my car being stolen. I had only left it on the street for a few minutes but, on my return, I saw two lads sitting in the front seats. How would you react? When you have no time to think, you find out what you're really like. Instinctively, I quickened my step, but tried not to attract their attention as they would know it was my car. My plan was instant: I would open the driver's door and punch him as hard as I could in the face and keep punching him until he couldn't resist. I went for the door handle. His reactions were quicker than mine. The engine was running, and he drove off, both wearing their seat belts.

Credit where credit's due. No sooner had they disappeared out of sight when I came to my senses, and thanked God the thief's reactions were quicker than mine. If I'd done what I had intended, I may have murdered him. That's forbidden in the sixth of God's Commandments, and that was the day it was confirmed to me that I had the seeds of murder deeply imbedded in my heart. I was shocked at how I had reacted. The car was old and not very reliable. I had never really liked it. I had no history of violence. The only fight I had been in was when I was about eleven years old, and a lad hit me, so I fought back. We tend to think we know our weaknesses, and I have many, but the shock to me was I didn't know instinctive violence was one of them.

Now this is serious because God can see all our thoughts and intentions and knows us better than we know ourselves. I was surprised by my reaction, but I know God wasn't.

Jesus reaffirms these Ten Commandments in his

God can see all our thoughts and intentions and knows us better than we know ourselves.

famous 'Sermon on the Mount', recorded in Matthew's Gospel. He makes it clear that God can see the inner workings of our heart and mind and is equally concerned about those as well as what we actually do. He says:

> You have heard that it was said to those of old, 'You shall not murder and whoever murders will be in danger of the judgement.' But I say to you that whoever is angry with his brother without a cause shall be in danger of the judgement (Matthew 5:21 and 22).

Now, stealing a car is a transgression against God. It crosses the line, so I definitely had a cause to be angry, but that anger wanted to keep hitting him until he could not resist. I don't think even the strictest law keeper would advocate the killing of a young lad for stealing an old car.

Jesus uses this, and the Seventh Commandment, 'You shall not commit adultery', as examples of God seeing our motives and intentions, saying, 'whoever looks at a woman to lust for her has already committed adultery with her in his heart' (Matthew 5:27, 28). God looks on our heart; there is our problem.

On another occasion, I went to visit someone in hospital

and unusually the car park was almost empty. I chose to park near the entrance next to another car. Perhaps being overconfident seeing so many spaces, I turned too quickly and dented the side of the other car before coming to a stop. Instinctively, I looked around to see if anyone had witnessed my stupidity. It was with relief that I saw no one was about and not a camera to be seen.

Again, we see in unexpected moments what we are really like. I don't think my reaction was unique. The first reaction is defensive. Had anyone seen? Maybe the first temptation is, 'Will anyone find out?' The moment I began to think it through, I knew what I ought to do. It was a fine day so I would put a note under their windscreen wipers so they couldn't miss it, giving my contact number and explaining I was responsible for the dent in their car, and for them to get in touch. I then went into the hospital reflecting on my mistake but comforted by the knowledge that I had done the right thing in leaving a note. In fact, the more I thought about it the more pleased with myself I became, knowing that many people would have taken the opportunity to drive away unseen, and yet, I did not.

I continued to feel good until I remembered that pride is particularly mentioned by God as something he hates. So, there I was. I had done the right thing but stank of pride in the process. That is the human heart. Even when we do something right, still the corruption of the human heart can be seen.

These examples are to bring home to us that sin is not to be thought of as 'just being human'—those isolated incidents in our weakest moments. It permeates everything. Understanding what our heart is really like, even though it is a painful process, is a massive step towards understanding what Christ came to do.

When one of our daughters was born, she was critically ill and needed to have open heart surgery. I remember vividly the doctor explaining the diagnosis and the necessary radical treatment. Obviously, it would have been a happier occasion if the doctor had said there is a medicine and after a few doses she'll be fine. But that wasn't an option. If she was to live, she needed open heart surgery. It was as simple as that.

In the same way, we can look at the problems of human beings and apply remedies all day long, but if we do not see the extent of the problem, we are using sticking plasters when we need surgery. After any reported atrocity, we often hear those in authority assuring us that new safeguarding measures, or new legislation will be put into place to ensure this will never happen again. It is, of course, right that any society should do all it can to prevent evil. But we recognize that no amount of safeguarding can address the root cause of our problems.

The apostle Paul tells us, 'The wages of sin is death, but the gift of God is eternal life in Christ Jesus our Lord' (Romans 6:23). Here we see the diagnosis. Sin is the biggest problem you and I have. We also see the prognosis. Death is described as the wages of sin. It is the inevitable consequence of our sin, and we have earned it!

Please pause here and think about what God tells us. If we compare ourselves with other people, we will see some better than ourselves but plenty worse. That is how most people come to terms with what they are, and they are pleased that they are not as bad as many others. But we are looking at God's standards, and they are the ones that matter. We shall be judged by him, and what other people think of us, or what we think about ourselves will not matter.

It is worth noting that these standards are still generally accepted throughout the world. My attention was caught a few years ago by a write up about a U.K. documentary entitled, 'The New Ten commandments'. Voters were asked to suggest a set of new commandments that were relevant to the way we live today. Although the write up concluded that the result was 'a comprehensive trashing of the old order', a closer look reveals otherwise. Jonathan Sacks, chief rabbi in the U.K. at the time, did not see them as a radical change from the past. He commented: 'Almost all the new commandments are back there in the Bible. The only really new one is "Be true to yourself."'[4] People the world over still think it's wrong to murder, steal and lie.

Our problem, even in our generation and for all

generations, is not being clueless as to what is right and wrong, but the insistence of our hearts to be drawn towards wrong. It is then we are in danger of turning to another alternative. We try to justify what is wrong, because that is really what we want to do. As the apostle Paul explains:

> Although they knew God, they did not glorify Him as God, nor were thankful, but became futile in their thoughts, and their foolish hearts were darkened. Professing to be wise, they became fools (Romans 1:21–22).

And isn't the new commandment, 'be true to yourself'? We follow our natural inclinations, wilfully denying God's definition of sin and his description of the human heart and saying, 'It feels so right, it can't be wrong.'

I remember hearing a celebrity, known for her intellect in the U.K., explaining why she left her husband for another man, and she simply said if she hadn't done so she would not have been 'true to herself'. This, in many parts of the world, is the sentiment of the day and has been for many decades. When we are told, as we often are, 'just be yourself,' we need to remember exactly what our self is like.

However, when we look at God's standard, we see how short of the mark we are. Our main problem with these commands, bearing in mind we are to keep them inwardly, is that we realize they are, in fact, impossible for us to keep. We may well ask, then, what is the point of setting a standard to which we cannot attain? The Bible gives us the explanation: the apostle Paul again says, 'by the law is the knowledge of sin' (Romans 3:20).

The chief purpose of these commandments is not only to direct our love, but to show us what we are really like. We are not, according to God's standard, even remotely good. The Bible tells us, 'All our righteousnesses are like filthy rags' (Isaiah 64:6).

A few 'monsters' are not the cause of the world's problems. You and I are. Quite simply we need help from outside our situation. Even a team of engineers trained in fixing broken lifts are of no use if they are stranded between floors in one. They, like us, need help from outside. Our hearts, the centre of our inner being, are not equipped for self-rescue.

A few 'monsters' are not the cause of the world's problems. You and I are.

Yet, there is a remedy offered from outside, and notice it is described as a gift; the gift of complete forgiveness and eternal life. So, let us now turn to the remedy on offer.

HOW CAN JESUS TAKE SIN AWAY?

John the Baptist tells us: Look! This Jesus is the one 'who takes away the sin of the world' (John 1:29). He will address our greatest problem and deal with it. That is what is being claimed. We have noted already that Jesus has many names given to him in the Bible. Here we have another one: 'the Lamb of God'. John the Baptist uses this extraordinary name referring to Jesus because it points us to how Jesus will set out to accomplish his task.

Lambs had a central role in the sacrificial system of the Old Testament and the people of Israel. Every morning and evening on a daily basis they were told to sacrifice a lamb. It had to be killed and its blood shed. Even before this, a central story in the history of Israel, often repeated, was when they had been freed as slaves from Egypt during the time of Moses. On that occasion also, a lamb was sacrificed, and they were told to commemorate this event on a yearly basis as the feast of Passover; and the lamb was referred to as the 'Passover lamb'.

Now this idea of killing an animal in some religious ceremony seems so alien to the modern mind, that we may be tempted to simply dismiss it as ignorance and be thankful we live in more enlightened times. But we need to be careful we do not miss the point of what was happening. We have learned that the Bible teaches the 'wages of sin is death' (Romans 6:23). We are also taught we are personally answerable to God and 'The soul who sins shall die' (Ezekiel 18:20).

That brings us back to our modern world. Death is a reality for all of us, just as it was for humans all those years ago. With all our medical, scientific and technological progress human beings have made over the years, we are not one step closer to solving the problem of death. Even though some would say we should not look on death as a problem but as an integral part of being human, for most of us their promise of a future of nothingness is still alien to our heart's aspirations and hopes. The reason is, 'He has put eternity in their hearts' (Ecclesiastes 3:11). We look for answers beyond death because that is how God made us.

We look for answers beyond death because that is how God made us.

The point of these sacrifices was to teach us we deserve to die because of our sin but, instead, God was willing to accept the death of a lamb in our place, as our substitute. It was not, however, the complete answer as, although we are told 'without shedding of blood there is no remission [forgiveness]' (Hebrews 9:22), we are also told, 'it is not possible that the blood of bulls and goats [also sacrificed as well as lambs] could take away sins' (Hebrews 10:4). It is the Bible book of Hebrews that explains why these animal sacrifices were to prepare the way for Jesus.

When John the Baptist points to Jesus as the 'Lamb of God', he is telling us that this man can do much more than those lambs, who for centuries had been killed instead of the sinful people who really deserved to die. They were thankful for such a provision, but killing an animal was never intended to be the final answer for the forgiveness of sins. They were merely pointing forward to the time when God would provide a sacrifice that really would take away sin.

John now points to Jesus and says the time has arrived. He is the one who will die instead of us and take the punishment we deserve. He will not only deal with the penalty of sin but, as we shall see, he will perfect and transform the whole of creation, including human beings. The book of Hebrews again explains the situation. Speaking of Jesus, it says:

> He has appeared to put away sin by the sacrifice of Himself. And as it is appointed for men to die once, but after this the judgement, so Christ was offered once to bear the sins of many (Hebrews 9:26–28).

The apostle Paul is even more specific in referring to Jesus and saying: 'For indeed Christ, our Passover [Lamb], was sacrificed for us' (1 Corinthians 5:7), while the apostle Peter refers to 'the precious blood of Christ, as of a lamb without blemish and without spot' (1 Peter 1:19).

This idea of Jesus standing in our place as a substitute and taking the punishment we deserve was Jesus' understanding of what he was doing. On the very night he was arrested and taken to be crucified, he told the disciples, 'All of you will be made to stumble because of Me this night, for it is written: "I will strike the Shepherd, and the sheep of the flock will be scattered"' (Matthew 26:31). When he was arrested that is exactly what happened, as his disciples left him and fled for their lives. But how did he know that would happen? His explanation was, 'for it is written'. He used that phrase and similar phrases a lot when referring to Scripture as his authority and, on this occasion, he was referring to the Old Testament prophet Zechariah:

> 'Awake, O sword, against My Shepherd, against the man who is My Companion,' says the LORD of hosts. 'Strike the Shepherd, and the sheep will be scattered' (Zechariah 13:7).

God is recorded here as saying he would take his sword of judgement to bring down on Jesus, who was described as his *shepherd* and *companion*, and that is why his sheep [the disciples] would be scattered. Jesus was expecting to take the place of those who deserved to be punished and be punished himself instead of them. In John's Gospel, Jesus teaches his disciples, 'Greater love has no one than this, than to lay down one's life for his friends' (John 15:13).

One of the reasons I was brought to believe in Jesus was that his teaching and life are in complete harmony. There are many teachers in the world who have fine ideas but cannot live according to their own teaching. Not so with Jesus, as the apostle Paul explains:

> But God demonstrates His own love toward us, in that while we were still sinners, Christ died for us. Much more then, having now been justified by His blood, we shall be saved from wrath through Him. For if when we were enemies we were reconciled to God through the death of His Son, much more, having been reconciled, we shall be saved by His life (Romans 5:8–10).

God is described as 'the justifier of the one who has faith in Jesus' (Romans 3:26). The word, 'justified', means God has not condemned us but acquitted us and declared us righteous. That has come about not because we are without guilt, but because Christ chose to die in our place.

On at least three separate occasions Jesus tells his disciples he must go to Jerusalem and there be crucified. He saw it as his assignment. It is what he had come to do. His very first introduction to us in the New Testament is recorded by the Gospel writers. Even before he was born, Joseph (Jesus' human father), who was due to marry Mary, was told:

> Joseph, son of David, do not be afraid to take to you Mary your wife, for that which is conceived in her is of the Holy Spirit. And she will bring forth a Son,

and you shall call His name JESUS, for He will save His people from their sins (Matthew 1:20-21).

The logic of that is the name Jesus like all his other names has a meaning, and the meaning is 'Saviour'.

The apostle Paul sums it up: 'This is a faithful saying and worthy of all acceptance, that Christ Jesus came into the world to save sinners' (1 Timothy 1:15). This was his assignment. To accomplish his assignment, he was to die as 'the Lamb of God' and thereby, take away the sin of the world. That is why he said at his last supper (often called communion), referring to the bread they were eating, 'This is My body which is given for you; do this in remembrance of Me.' And referring to the wine, he said, 'This cup is the new covenant in My blood, which is shed for you' (Luke 22:19–20). He was voluntarily giving his body, and shedding his blood for others, as the Lamb of God, in their place, as their substitute. This was Jesus' understanding of how he would accomplish the assignment given to him. In paying the price we owe because of our sin, he would save sinners from the consequence and the enslavement of their transgressions.

When I first heard this message, I wondered how it could be that someone else could take the punishment that I deserved. It wasn't long before I understood. I had a close friend who I had known from school days. At home, he had nothing to cook on, so we decided it was time to get an oven. He chose one and arranged to pay for it on a monthly basis. His finances, however, were such that before he paid his first instalment he was asked to provide evidence to guarantee he could pay the full amount; he couldn't. That is where his friend came in. He signed an agreement as the guarantor. He would be responsible if the monthly payments did not arrive. He signed the agreement with full knowledge that the likelihood was he would probably end up footing the bill. That's how it turned out. He paid the bill, and his friend got his oven. Now I understood what Jesus did for me. I owed God, but Jesus paid the price.

In many societies, the desire for individualism can obscure how interrelated and connected we really are. We have seen some examples already demonstrating Jesus' world view was that of the Bible. So, he, like the rest of the Bible, holds that Adam, the first man, was a real person created by God. The apostle Paul is referring to Adam when he says:

> Through one man sin entered the world, and death through sin, and thus death spread to all men, because all sinned (Romans 5:12).

Our first parents' choices, we are told, affected all of us enormously, whether we like it or not. Adam, choosing to disobey God as he did, is the story of one individual who had a massive effect on every human being who has lived since, because he was representative of every human being, and we are connected and related to him. The apostle Paul goes on to liken the role of Adam to that of Jesus, when he says:

> For as by one man's disobedience many were made sinners, so also by one Man's obedience many will be made righteous (Romans 5:19).

Christ's death is much more than one person's experience, as he represents every person connected and related to him, so they can enjoy the benefits that flow from his obedience. We shall see a little later, how it is faith that makes us related and connected to him.

Do not underestimate the extent of your sin and transgressions against God. But neither underestimate his love for sinners. Jesus, we are told came into the world to save sinners. Understand you are one, and he is immediately relevant. If, however, you are of the opinion that you have always loved God and your neighbour perfectly and believe you will be found innocent on the judgement day, I understand why you will not be interested in Jesus. He only came for sinners. Jesus himself said:

Do not underestimate the extent of your sin and transgressions against God. But neither underestimate his love for sinners.

Those who are well have no need for a physician, but those who are sick. I did not come to call the righteous, but sinners, to repentance (Mark 2:17).

Notes

1 Gobodo-Madikizela, Pumla, *A Human Being Died that Night*, (London: Portobello Books Ltd., 2006), p. 32.

2 Ibid., p. 34.

3 Ibid., Preface.

4 This was a documentary by Jon Snow for Channel 4. It is no longer accessible on their website.

3 How does the world respond to God visiting us?

The Gospel of John, chapter 1, verses 10 and 11 says:

He was in the world, and the world was made through Him, and the world did not know Him. He came to His own, and His own did not receive Him.

John's eyewitness account of Jesus told us he was the Word, God himself, and the Creator, who had life in himself. John the Baptist's account informed us Jesus Christ had come to take away the sin of the world. How did the people of the day respond?

Well, it appears many simply did not recognize him! I can't help but think of when I used to say, 'I don't think there is enough evidence to believe there is a God.' But what if God actually visited this planet, albeit two thousand years ago, and he simply was not recognized?

I have seen and met famous people myself and did not know who they were, and I suspect many people have had the same experience. I was at the Great Yorkshire show with one of my daughters when we passed the media tent, and I saw a number of people outside talking. My daughter commented after passing, mentioning all the famous people she had seen. 'Why didn't you tell me?' I asked. 'I knew you wouldn't know any of them,' was her response. I couldn't argue with her. I am not an avid film watcher and could probably count the number of people who I know as famous 'celebrities' on a couple of hands.

I also once had a conversation with a delightful couple on the tube in London who apparently were the biggest names in Bollywood. As my stop had arrived, I said goodbye and squeezed through a crowd of excited people, busy taking photos. I was only told who they were after asking a bemused onlooker who had assumed I was a friend because we had been in close conversation. Not recognizing famous people is, I suspect, quite common. But John is telling us that God himself visited this planet and lived among us and was not recognized. Is that possible?

It is entirely possible when we consider a couple of factors.

The first factor is the manner in which he came and his lifestyle. The birth of Jesus is certainly memorable because of the circumstances surrounding it. Two very young, poor people, Joseph and Mary, have to lay their firstborn baby in a feeding trough for animals, because they had no accommodation.

After a period in Egypt, because they had to flee to escape King Herod murdering the child, they returned to Nazareth where Jesus was brought up. It was a byword among the people of the day: 'Can anything good come out of Nazareth?' (John 1:46). He then worked as a carpenter, until he began touring the towns and villages preaching about the kingdom of God. His situation was such that he commented to his disciples that, 'Foxes have holes and birds of the air have nests, but the Son of Man [another name for Jesus, and his preference when referring to himself] has nowhere to lay His head' (Luke 9:58). He then announced that he must go to Jerusalem where he would be crucified. And that is what happened.

It was not a life which fitted the expectations for the coming Messiah. Many had expected a king who would drive out the occupying Roman army and restore the nation of Israel to its halcyon days of King David. But this man, Jesus, had other priorities which ran contrary to expectation. This is the second factor that they, perhaps like our generation, were looking for God according to their own expectations and to fulfil their own desires without taking into account God's agenda. Human beings do not consider their own heart as the fundamental problem in our world, so why would they be looking to God to solve a problem they didn't even know they had?

Having said that, when John says, 'He came to His own, and His own did not receive Him, he is not simply talking about the Creator coming to those he has created. These were the people to which 'the law and the prophets' had been given. The Old Testament, with its central theme of preparing a people for the coming of the Messiah, had made clear he would come to deal with the sin problem. The Bible passages of Psalm 22 and Isaiah 53, both written hundreds of years before Jesus, give extraordinary detail of the suffering the coming Messiah would endure.

But when we remember the hearts' ability to suppress truth, and its innate opposition to God, it is entirely understandable how God himself came into this world and was not recognized and received. The apostle Paul summarizes Jesus' attitude and lifestyle:

> Let this mind [attitude] be in you which was also in Christ Jesus, who, being in the form of God, did not consider it robbery to be equal with God, but made Himself of no reputation [made himself nothing], taking the form of a bondservant [the lowliest of servants], and coming in the likeness of men. And being found in appearance as a man, He humbled Himself and became obedient to the point of death, even the death of the cross (Philippians 2:5–8).

The world was expecting something else. Certainly not someone who would humble himself, make himself nothing and die on a cross!

The world was expecting something else. Certainly

not someone who would humble himself, make himself nothing and die on a cross!

Yet, as well as the Old Testament Scriptures, to show who he was, Jesus himself provided evidence. To help people believe in Jesus, the Gospel writer, John, records seven of what have become some of the best-known miracles of Jesus, including turning water into wine; walking on water; and bringing Lazarus, who had been dead for four days, back to life. All these are recorded as actual historic events witnessed by John. They are presented to us as evidence Jesus provided that he is who he says. Jesus said:

> The works that I do in my Father's name, they bear witness of Me ... If I do not do the works of My Father, do not believe Me; but if I do, though you do not believe Me, believe the works, that you may know and believe that the Father is in Me, and I in Him (John 10:25, 37–38).

He refers to his miracles as 'the works' he is doing and points to them as evidence. This seems quite ironic in our generation as many people do not take Jesus' claims seriously—not despite his miracles, but because of them. They simply believe such miracles including a resurrection are impossible, so the whole story must be false.

In a similar situation, Jesus was once confronted

by people who found it impossible to believe that resurrection could ever be a reality:

> Jesus answered and said to them, 'You are mistaken, not knowing the Scriptures nor the power of God. ... Have you not read what was spoken to you by God, saying, "I am the God of Abraham, the God of Isaac, and the God of Jacob?" God is not the God of the dead, but of the living' (Matthew 22:29, 31–32).

If we rely only on our experience, any thought of resurrection can be immediately dismissed. But Jesus pointed to the teaching of Scripture, because he knew it to be true, and to the power of God. If something seems impossible to us, he urges us to remember, like Mary, 'with God nothing will be impossible' (Luke 1:37).

Jesus, however, insisted he did these miracles so people would recognize who he was. If it is true that God is real and visited this planet 2,000 years ago in the person of Jesus, what do you think he could do to make himself known? When he was dying on the cross, one of the taunts aimed at him was:

> He saved others; Himself He cannot save. If He is the King of Israel, let Him now come down from the cross, and we will believe Him (Matthew 27:42).

That was the challenge given by the chief priests, the scribes and elders, and all the religious leaders of the day. They had made their own minds up concerning what it would take for them to believe in Jesus. The great problem for them, and for people of a similar mind today, is failing to see the evidence Jesus gives and insisting on their own demands being met. What if Jesus had done what they requested for the sake of a few more disciples? The answer to that is he would not have accomplished his assignment. He would not, as the Lamb of God, have taken away the sin of the world.

One modern dramatist came up with the idea of a shaft of light piercing the night sky to miraculously illuminate a football ground without the aid of floodlights. Surely that would convince people. What Jesus chose to do was to walk on water, bring back the dead and be resurrected himself.

The religious leaders, who were the enemies of Jesus, could not deny miracles were happening, but resorted to telling people he was doing this through the power of the devil and not God. Jesus, however, was providing real evidence. As Luke says,

> He also presented Himself alive after His suffering by many infallible proofs, being seen by them during forty days and speaking of the things pertaining to the kingdom of God (Acts 1:3).

He was not trying to be secretive or allusive, and God was not playing 'hide and seek'. He is there for anyone who wants to take notice!

4 What does it mean to believe in Jesus?

The Gospel of John, chapter 1, verse 12 says:

But as many as received Him, to them He gave the right to become children of God, to those who believe in His name:

John now tells us that not everyone rejected Jesus but some 'received Him' and 'believed in His name'. These, we are told, are the people who were given 'the right to become children of God'.

WHAT IS MEANT BY RECEIVING JESUS AND BELIEVING IN HIS NAME?

When reading through the Gospels of Matthew, Mark and Luke it becomes evident that one incident recorded by all of them was massively important to Jesus. It was the occasion when Jesus asked his disciples, 'Who do men say I, the Son of Man, am?' A number of answers were given until Jesus asked:

> 'But who do you say that I am?' Simon Peter answered and said, 'You are the Christ, the Son of the living God.' Jesus answered and said to him, 'Blessed are you, Simon Bar-Jonah, for flesh and blood has not revealed this to you, but My Father who is in heaven' (Matthew 16:13–17).

Up until this point, it seemed one of the main objectives for Jesus had been to convince the disciples of who he was. Peter appears to be speaking on behalf of all of them when he identifies Jesus as 'the Christ'. The disciples had, in effect, 'received' Jesus Christ.

In the same passage in Matthew, we read of other people who were trying to work out who Jesus was. Some thought he may be one of the great prophets from the past, and suggested Jeremiah or Elijah may have come back. Even John the Baptist, now dead, was mentioned as a possibility. These people obviously had a very high view and respect for Jesus to suggest he may be one of the national heroes from the past.

But Jesus passed by those ideas without comment because he wanted to hear what the disciples thought. He answered Peter by saying he was a blessed man to truly recognize he was the Christ. He also pointed out that God himself had revealed the truth of his identity to him. As far as Jesus was concerned, they had 'received' him for who he was.

This appears to be the chief criteria which defines a true disciple and Christian: the recognition of the identity of Jesus through his name. He is the Christ, named twice by Isaiah and quoted in Matthew's Gospel as 'Immanuel', which means 'God with us' (Matthew 1:23). His disciples had recognized him for who he is: the man who is God.

The other word used by John, the Gospel writer, to

differentiate between those who did not receive Jesus and those who did is, 'believe'; 'Those who believe in His name.' We have noticed some of the names of Jesus, and all of them are significant. This again focuses on the idea that believing in Jesus is first of all to recognize his true identity as expressed in 'His name'. 'Receiving' and 'believing' amount to the same thing in this passage but the word, 'believe', is chiefly used in Scripture as the response Jesus was looking for. It means all that is required of us is to trust Jesus himself and his message, because of who he is.

When I first heard this, I thought I had missed something. Surely, I thought, if we are to become God's children and receive forgiveness, we have to do something to earn it. It took a while to sink in that Christ himself had done everything necessary for us.

The most helpful illustration of Christ perfectly accomplishing his assignment to save sinners, I have come across, is of a farmer who needed a new gate to his field. He hired the best carpenter he knew to do the job, and he finished his work to the complete satisfaction of the farmer. It was the best gate he had on his land, and he thought it was perfect.

This same farmer had been thinking about Jesus and Christianity and had often talked to a local Christian who had explained Christ had done everything that needed to be done. All we have to do is trust him and believe in him.

The farmer, however, could never really grasp this, and thought he must do something to earn God's favour. He had told his friend how pleased he was with the new gate and how perfect it was. This gave his friend an idea.

So, he boldly told the farmer he would bring his tools and fix the gate the next day. The reply was, 'It does not need fixing, it is perfect, don't try to alter this gate.' Nevertheless, his friend insisted he would be up early the next morning to improve the gate.

The next morning the farmer was up before dawn to make sure he was at the gate before his determined friend. He didn't have long to wait before his friend arrived with his hammer, nails, and chisel. 'There is nothing wrong with this gate,' said the farmer. 'It is perfect. Don't you dare try to make it better by adding to it, you will only spoil it.'

'If that is true,' said his friend, 'why are you trying to improve Christ's accomplishments by insisting on adding your paltry efforts to improve them? There is nothing wrong with Christ's accomplishments, they are perfect. Don't you dare try to make them better by adding to them, you will only spoil them. His death on the cross accomplished everything we need.' What this farmer needed to understand was all that was required of him was to trust Jesus, because Jesus had done it all.

Jesus was once asked a question:

> 'Who then is greatest in the kingdom of heaven?' Then Jesus called a little child to Him, set him in the midst of them, and said, 'Assuredly, I say to you, unless you are converted and become as little children, you will by no means enter the kingdom of heaven. Therefore, whoever humbles himself as this little child is the greatest in the kingdom of heaven' (Matthew 18:1–4).

Jesus was not asking us to be childish, but to be childlike when it comes to humility and trust.

Jesus was not asking us to be childish, but to be childlike when it comes to humility and trust.

I saw a great example of this when I watched a father and his two sons on a beach on the east coast of Yorkshire. The two lads had climbed from the beach to the promenade above, and the father had shouted, 'Jump back down and I will catch you.' The youngest of the children beamed with delight, went back some distance so he could run as fast as he could and leap towards his dad's outstretched arms. He launched himself from the promenade star shaped, arms out, legs out, with no plan 'B'. If his dad had not caught him, it would not have been a pretty sight; he would have landed nose first and tears would have followed. This 'little child' had complete confidence in his dad, and his confidence was justified. His dad, true to his word, caught him and they celebrated together.

This is what Jesus is calling us to do. Trust me. Leave your plan 'B' behind. Get rid of it. Ditch it.

Now it was the older son's turn. He could not be described as a 'little child' and he was not as confident his dad would catch him. So, he ran towards his dad's outstretched arms, but you could tell immediately he had a plan 'B' and possibly even a plan 'C'. No star shape here, but a jump towards his dad, making sure he would land on his feet if his dad did not grab him. This made it very difficult for his dad, who nearly caught him but not quite because the older lad was making sure he landed on his feet.

Jesus' teaching is wonderful in its detail. He did not ask an older child to stand in their midst; it was a younger child, because they are capable of complete trust. When Jesus invites us to believe in him, that is what he is asking: 'You recognize who I am. Now trust me.' The little lad trusted his dad because he was his dad, but he proved it by doing what he asked. That is what Jesus is asking. Believe in me, because of who I am, and prove it by doing what I ask.

WHAT DOES JESUS ASK US TO DO?

What, then, does Jesus require from those who believe in him? We shall look at this in more detail a little later, but a good place to start is by referring to Mark's Gospel, which tells us:

> Jesus came to Galilee, preaching the gospel of the kingdom of God and saying, 'The time is fulfilled, and the kingdom of God is at hand. Repent, and believe in the gospel' (Mark 1:14–15).

Here, Jesus is saying that the long wait for the Messiah is over. He has arrived. He made the same point at his hometown synagogue in Nazareth, when he read the opening verses of Isaiah, chapter 61, which says:

> The Spirit of the LORD is upon Me, because He has anointed Me to preach the gospel to the poor; He has sent Me to heal the broken-hearted, to proclaim liberty to the captives and recovery of sight to the blind, to set at liberty those who are oppressed; to proclaim the acceptable year of the LORD (Luke 4:18–19).

He then, applies this Scripture directly to himself and tells the congregation, 'Today this Scripture is fulfilled in your hearing' (Luke 4:21). He was declaring the arrival of God's kingdom with the coming of the Messiah, God's appointed king. But the verse in Mark tells us exactly what he asks us to do: 'Repent and believe in the gospel (1:15).

The word, 'gospel', simply means 'good news'. It is the good news of Jesus coming into this world to be our Saviour, and accomplishing everything Isaiah prophesied about the Messiah: for the broken hearted to be healed, for genuine freedom, and the sight of understanding. It is the most glorious news we can ever hear in this world and there is no other message which remotely compares to the hope offered here. To 'believe in the gospel' therefore, is to trust Jesus and the message he brings.

For anything to be called 'good news', it has to be part of a bigger story. If someone tells you to enjoy your day because you are not going to prison for the next twenty years, how you receive that news entirely depends on the context. Tell it to a law-abiding friend who has never been in trouble with the police, and they will give you a quizzical look, and say, 'That's nice to know but I had no expectations of needing to go to jail in the first place.' But tell it to the person who has just finished a trial for murder and been found not guilty, and that is really good news.

The gospel is 'good news' within a bigger story, and that story is the world view of Jesus and the Bible. In a nutshell:

- God is the Creator. He made us and we are answerable to him.
- He is righteous (perfect) in all his ways. We are sinners (unrighteous).
- We are separated from God and guilty before Him. We are told 'it is appointed for men to die once, but after this the judgement' (Hebrews 9:27).
- Heaven and hell are a reality. We are heading for

judgement and hell unless we can be saved from the consequences of our sin.

We need to be clear that this summary is the world view of Jesus. Matthew, another eyewitness, records Jesus as saying:

> When the Son of Man comes in His glory, and all the holy angels with Him, then He will sit on the throne of His glory. All the nations will be gathered before Him, and He will separate them one from another, as a shepherd divides his sheep from the goats. And He will set the sheep on His right hand, but the goats on the left (Matthew 25:31–33).

When Jesus came to this earth, his mission was to save sinners. He tells us here he will return to this earth but, next time, will return as the judge. The passage in Matthew goes on to explain how he will separate the nations into two groups of people, pictured here as the sheep and the goats.

Our world likes to differentiate between people in many different ways: black, white; east, west; political left and right; Jew, gentile; male, female, sexual orientation and so on. But Jesus has only two categories on judgement day. He ends by telling us the outcome:

> Then the King will say to those on His right hand, 'Come you blessed of My Father, inherit the kingdom prepared for you from the foundation

> of the world: for I was hungry and you gave Me food; I was thirsty and you gave Me drink; I was a stranger and you took Me in; I was naked and you clothed Me; I was sick and you visited Me; I was in prison and you came to Me.' Then the righteous will answer Him, saying 'Lord, when did we see You hungry and feed you, or thirsty and give You drink? When did we see You a stranger and take You in, or naked and clothe You? Or when did we see You sick, or in prison, and come to You?' And the King will answer and say to them, 'Assuredly, I say to you, inasmuch as you did it to one of the least of these My brethren, you did it to Me' (Matthew 25:34–40).

Those on his right hand (the sheep) were accepted because they believed in Jesus and proved it by doing what he had asked them to do. They had shown love for 'the least of these My brethren'. Those on his left (the goats) were not accepted. He concludes by saying, 'And these [the goats] will go away into everlasting punishment, but the righteous [the sheep] into eternal life' (Matthew 25:46). As far as Jesus is concerned, he presents this coming event of judgement as a reality.

It is into this bigger story, that the gospel is set. Our situation is presented as serious, and it is in this context that Jesus brings his message, recorded for us by Mark 1:15: 'Repent and believe in the gospel.'

Like John the Baptist before him, Jesus' message was for us to repent. That was his message at the start of his ministry, all the way through his ministry and at the end of his ministry. It is astonishing that so many churches have completely dropped this message from their agenda. Jesus, however, insists we are not only to recognize and acknowledge that we have failed to love God and our neighbour as we ought, but then to repent, changing our minds to accept Jesus as our Lord.

When a rich young ruler came to Jesus, as recorded in Mark 10:17–22, he asked, "Good teacher what shall I do that I may inherit eternal life?' Jesus' answer was to tell him about the righteousness of God: that only he was good. He then quoted five of the Ten Commandments and when the young man, thinking only the outward keeping of the commandments mattered, said, 'Teacher, all these things I have kept from my youth,' Mark tells us, 'Jesus, looking at him, loved him.' The compassion of Christ was evident and was proved by him telling this young man the truth.

He put his finger on this man's problem. It was not simply because he was rich, but the fact that his wealth had now become his god, for which he was living. Jesus applied the command to repent by saying:

> 'Sell whatever you have and give to the poor, and

> you will have treasure in heaven; and come, take up your cross and follow Me' (Mark 10:21).

The man left sad and sorrowful, for he had 'great possessions'. Jesus would not compromise the truth. Because he loved him, the young man needed to know the truth. Repentance was essential.

When we understand it is our own sin which has caused our separation from God, it causes sorrow, and a desire to change. He is asking us to change our mind about God and acknowledge our sin is a personal affront to him. We pray to him and ask him for forgiveness. For some people, this may be the first time they have ever prayed from their heart. They can, however, pray with confidence, knowing the message of the gospel—that, 'God so loved the world that He gave His only begotten Son, that whoever believes in Him should not perish but have everlasting life'—has become the best news possible. It is because we now understand the context, the bigger story. If you desire eternal life, this is one thing you must do: you must repent of your sins. We are not ignorant of what sin is.

God makes it known. Acknowledge it, confess it, turn from it and God is willing to forgive.

WHAT BENEFITS COME TO THOSE WHO BELIEVE IN JESUS?

John says, for those who receive and believe in Jesus, God gives them 'the right to become the children of God'.

The Bible speaks of many benefits for those who believe in Jesus, including eternal life. The word, 'saved', is also frequently used, referring to us being saved from the consequences and the power of sin, and saved from the wrath of God both now and on judgement day. But John is content to tell us about just one benefit. It is how God adopts everyone who believes in his only begotten Son, and perhaps the reason he chooses this is that every other benefit flows from it.

I have often heard the expression, 'We are all God's children,' said by people with good intentions who are trying to make the point that there should be no divisions between human beings. When God tells us we are to 'love our neighbour,' it is inclusive of every individual, whoever they are, so the desire to emphasize this is commendable.

The apostle Paul, when preaching at Athens, is also keen to emphasize how we must not set human beings against each other through false divisions. He says, 'He [God] has made from one blood every nation of men to dwell on all the face of the earth,' and then quotes an Athenian poet, agreeing with him when he says, 'For we are also His offspring' (Acts 17:26, 28).

John here, makes it clear that being the offspring of God is, however, not the same as being adopted. To be a child of God requires, firstly, adoption and, as John points out, that comes through receiving and believing in Christ.

The apostle Paul also tells us this adoption is for people

who believe in Christ: 'For you are all sons of God through faith in Jesus Christ (Galatians 3:26). Here, 'faith' is the word used to express the trust and confidence a believing person has in Jesus. It is what connects us and unites us with Christ. Faith begins with knowing who Christ is, and his gospel message. The apostle Paul tells us:

'Faith' is the word used to express the trust and confidence a believing person has in Jesus. It is what connects us and unites us with Christ.

> Whoever calls on the name of the LORD shall be saved. How then shall they call on Him in whom they have not believed? And how shall they believe in Him of whom they have not heard? And how shall they hear without a preacher? ... So then faith comes by hearing, and hearing by the word of God (Romans 10:13–14, 17).

It is when this information has been communicated that a person is then in a position to either believe or reject Jesus' claims. Faith is when the message of Christ and his gospel are believed as true. But there is one more aspect to faith, as James tells us:

> You believe that there is one God. You do well. Even the demons believe—and tremble! But do you want

> to know, O foolish man, that faith without works is dead? (James 2:19–20).

Faith is not a mere intellectual assent to Christ and his message but needs to be acted upon.

If you are in a building and someone runs into the room, urgently shouting, 'Get out, the building is on fire,' you would not need to ask for a show of hands to find out who thought their message was true. You would see immediately those who believed it was true because they would be heading for the exit and urging others to do so. The illustration of the young lad at the beach serves us well, as he trusted his dad to catch him because he was his dad, but he showed it by doing exactly what his dad had asked. Faith then, is knowing certain facts, believing them, and trusting God as our Father by doing what he asks.

Paul goes on to say:

> When the fullness of the time had come, God sent forth His Son, born of a woman, born under the law, to redeem those who were under the law, that we might receive the adoption as sons. And because you are sons, God has sent forth the Spirit of His Son into your hearts, crying out, 'Abba, Father!' (Galatians 4:4–6).

'*Abba*' is an Aramaic word and a slightly more informal expression of 'Father', used to express a Christian's new relationship with God as an adopted child. Paul is making the point that the believer's new-found relationship with God is a felt experience.

I once heard someone telling us about an embarrassing situation he had as a teenager. His father had died a few years before, and his mother had remarried. Her new husband was keen to play the father's role for his stepson and asked him if he could call him 'Father', as he would refer to him as his son. As he liked his new dad, he tried hard to comply with his wishes. The only problem was that he had clear memories of his actual dad who had died, so calling his mum's new husband, 'Dad', did not come naturally. He made every effort to remember, but was trying so hard, he accidentally called his teacher at school, 'Dad', which led to months of mockery from his friends.

What Paul is telling us here, is that the believer's adoption into God's family does not involve us having to try hard to remember God is now our Father, but we experience his presence and kindness towards us as his children.

It is this experience in relationship with God through faith, which confirms to us that Jesus and his gospel are true. Jesus put it like this:

> If anyone wills to do His will, he shall know concerning the doctrine, whether it is from God or whether I speak on My own authority (John 7:17).

He implies here that we will never come to a decision about whether Jesus is telling the truth until we choose to do God's will. We are then brought back to the same question: 'What does God want us to do?' When asked a similar question, Jesus said, 'This is the work of God, that you believe in Him whom He sent' (John 6:29). Jesus always insisted he had been sent by God, and here, he tells us that God's will for us is to trust the one he has sent. In doing so, the believer in Jesus has the felt experience of their adoption into God's family confirming to them Jesus and his message are 'from God'.

THIS MESSAGE OF REPENTANCE AND BELIEVING IN JESUS CONTINUES FOR EACH GENERATION

Jesus had told his disciples, on a number of occasions, that he must go to Jerusalem and there be crucified. He also told them that three days after his death he would be resurrected. The disciples understandably found this hard to take in but still continued to follow him. After the event, however, each one of them was convinced that Jesus was truly alive and claimed they had seen him, spoken to him and even eaten with him over a period of forty days.

I mention this now because the last instructions he gave to his disciples before returning to his Father in heaven, was 'to go and make disciples of all the nations' (Matthew 28:19). He gave them the task of passing on his message to future generations and told them to wait first in Jerusalem where they would receive the gift of the Holy Spirit.

It was at the annual feast of Pentecost, fifty days after his crucifixion and ten days after he ascended into heaven, that the followers of Jesus were met together, and the Holy Spirit came upon them. Jerusalem was full of people from different nations and many different languages were represented. The Holy Spirit miraculously enabled the followers of Jesus to speak in the languages and dialects of those present, so people from different parts of the world could hear and understand them speaking about the wonderful works of God.

A crowd gathered and the apostle Peter explained what was happening. He told the people gathered who Jesus was, and how he had been crucified but now God had raised him up, so he was enthroned in heaven:

> 'God has made this Jesus, whom you crucified, both Lord and Christ.' Now when they heard this, they were cut to the heart, and said to Peter and the rest of the apostles, 'Men and brethren, what shall we do?' Then Peter said to them, 'Repent, and let everyone of you be baptized in the name of Jesus Christ for the remission [forgiveness] of sins; and you shall receive the gift of the Holy Spirit.' (Acts 2:36–38).

Approximately 3,000 of them did, and they continued

together to hear and follow the teaching of the apostles. They considered themselves brothers and sisters, as they had been adopted by God and met often to remember Christ's death and to pray, sharing as a family whatever anyone had need of.

The message Peter brought was the one Jesus had given. Recognize who Jesus is; trust him, and repent. The emphasis for the young church was the cross and resurrection of Christ. His assignment was now accomplished. He had set out to 'save sinners' and his mission was completed to perfection. The task now was for the apostles to pass the message on, so that others may believe and receive eternal life. They did so by proclaiming his crucifixion and resurrection from the dead.

Paul sums up the good news message when he is writing to the church in Corinth:

> I declare to you the gospel which I preached to you, which also you received and in which you stand, by which also you are saved, if you hold fast that word which I preached to you—unless you believed in vain.
>
> For I delivered to you first of all that which I also received: that Christ died for our sins according to the Scriptures, and that He was buried, and that He rose again the third day according to the Scriptures, and that He was seen by Cephas, then

> by the twelve. After that He was seen by over five hundred brethren at once, of whom the greater part remain to the present, but some have fallen asleep. After that He was seen by James, then by all the apostles. Then last of all He was seen by me also, as by one born out of due time (1 Corinthians 15:1–8).

The apostle Paul here gives a summary of 'the gospel'—the good news message, which the newly formed church was expected to pass to all the nations on earth. He was adamant that this message alone was the good news. When some churches stopped teaching this gospel, he wrote to them saying:

> I marvel that you are turning away so soon from Him who called you in the grace of Christ, to a different gospel, which is not another; but there are some who trouble you and want to pervert the gospel of Christ. But even if we, or an angel from heaven, preach any other gospel to you than what we have preached to you, let him be accursed (Galatians 1:6–8).

The strong language Paul uses here, emphasizes the 'gospel' that had been given was not intended as a starting point to develop another message contrary to Christ's death, burial, and resurrection. Believe in Christ, and 'the gospel' is the continuing message for a good reason as it is described as 'the power of God to salvation for everyone who believes' (Romans 1:16). It is this gospel which transforms lives for the good. It is one of the saddest things imaginable when churches change this gospel for another one as they never observe God working powerfully through the good news message.

The message of the resurrection of Christ then, became a central theme; the apostle Paul made it clear that 'if you confess with your mouth the Lord Jesus and believe in your heart that God has raised Him from the dead, you will be saved' (Romans 10:9).

It was this message that particularly affected me as a young man. I had always thought this idea of a resurrection was a made-up story that some people found inspirational. I had never seriously thought about whether it had actually happened or not. But I realized if it is a historic reality, Jesus must be accepted for who he says he is, and considered our Lord who can be trusted and followed. If he did not come back from the dead, everything he ever said falls to the ground. The apostle Paul put it like this: 'If Christ is not risen, your faith is futile; you are still in your sins!' (1 Corinthians 15:17).

This is why all the gospel writers take care to present the accounts of his resurrection appearances, after his death, as historic evidence. There are at least twelve accounts recorded in the New Testament where people said they had seen the risen Jesus, beginning with a group of women who had been followers of Jesus, and then to the disciples who had been with him throughout his ministry, to an occasion when over 500 people saw him at the one time.

The belief that Jesus had come back alive was not based on stories passed on from one generation to another which were elaborated over time. The people who said he was alive were those who claimed to have seen him with their own eyes.

I remember once hearing someone on the radio using a quote from Jock Stein, manager of Celtic football club, in the 1960s and 70s. I, along with many listeners, recognized the quote but remembered it was Bill Shankly, the manager of Liverpool F.C., who had said it, not Jock Stein. I wondered if the speaker would get away with it. He didn't, as the following day an apology was given due to the many people who had contacted the programme to point out the error. We were alive at the time. We had heard Bill Shankly ourselves and could testify they were his words.

Another important factor for me when I first began to look into the accounts of the resurrection was how those who said they had seen Jesus did not waver in their testimony. Charles W. Colson was an aide to President Richard Nixon and pleaded guilty to his involvement in the notorious Watergate scandal of 1972. He later became a Christian, and explained why he had come to believe in the resurrection of Jesus, in a now famous quote:

> I know the resurrection is a fact, and Watergate proved it to me. How? Because 12 men testified they had seen Jesus raised from the dead, then they proclaimed that truth for 40 years, never once denying it. Every one was beaten, tortured, stoned and put in prison. They would not have endured that if it weren't true. Watergate embroiled 12 of the most powerful men in the world and they couldn't keep a lie for three weeks. You're telling me 12 apostles could keep a lie for 40 years? Absolutely impossible.[1]

The impressive thing about the resurrection accounts is how diverse they are. When I was young, a group of us got interested in ghosts. We sometimes set out when it was dark and toured the graveyards and old streets of our area looking for 'spooks'. On every occasion, we came back thinking we had seen or heard something which made us certain they were out there. Why? Because we expected to see or hear something, so we always did.

The thing that impressed me about the appearances of Jesus after his resurrection was that they were not from a distance, in the dark, reported by people who expected to see something. None of the followers of Jesus were expecting this. They were people whose first reaction was one of fear at what they saw.

Thomas refused to believe that such a thing could happen even when his best and most trusted friends insisted they had seen Jesus. He hadn't, so he could not believe in such a thing. He had to wait until he had seen Jesus for himself before he said, 'My Lord, and my God' (John 20:28).

Jesus is recorded as appearing to different people, at different times, over a period of forty days, and speaking with these people. It is a long way from my childhood experience of insisting we saw or heard something 'spooky' (we soon grew out of it). But the resurrection of Jesus cannot so easily be explained away.

As a young man, reading through the Gospels for the first time, it became more apparent that, although the Bible's world view and especially the miracles recorded were alien to me, the message was not illogical or unreasonable. Jesus is not asking for us to have a 'blind faith' without any evidence and contrary to reason. But he is asking for faith in him, and his message.

Jesus is not asking for us to have a 'blind faith' without any evidence and contrary to reason. But he is asking for faith in him, and his message.

There came a time when I took my first faltering steps

towards prayer: 'God, if you are there, will you make yourself known?' Not a great prayer, but a start; and God is patient and kind and knows our thoughts and hearts. Wherever you are on your journey towards God, there comes a time when you need to pray. I experienced what every new convert to Christ experiences. I was being drawn towards God, which culminated in me finding faith in my heart to believe. This was a shock to me, and to all who knew me. I was not the type.

Why would I? John explains in his next verse.

Notes

1 www.goodreads.com/quotes/555921-i-know-the-resurrection-is-a-fact-and-watergate-proved

5 The need to be born again

The Gospel of John, chapter 1, verses 12 and 13 says:

But as many as received Him, to them He gave the right to become children of God, to those who believe in His name: who were born, not of blood, nor of the will of the flesh, nor of the will of man, but of God.

We move on now from verse 12 to verse 13, where John tells us how it can be that someone becomes a child of God. We mentioned briefly in the first chapter that Jesus taught: 'Unless one is born again, he cannot see the kingdom of God' (John 3:3). John now makes it clear that those who believe in Jesus are the very same as those who are born again and adopted. If one of those statements applies to us, then so do the other two. To be physically alive means we have obviously been born; this we have all experienced. But the Bible speaks of a second birth—one that is spiritual and brings us into a relationship with God.

But we cannot think of this spiritual birth in exactly the same way as a natural birth. John tells us this birth is not to do with our ancestry, race, or roots. Some people at the time of Jesus thought they were accepted by God because they were descended from Abraham, the Father of the nation. But Jesus makes it clear, as John does here when he says, 'not of blood', that ancestry is of no relevance to the spiritual birth. For by a natural birth through a physical relationship and sexual desire, a child is born, but we are told by Jesus that this second birth, which is spiritual, comes about through the Holy Spirit:

> That which is born of the flesh is flesh, and that which is born of the Spirit is spirit. Do not marvel that I said to you, 'You must be born again.' The wind blows where it wishes, and you hear the sound of it, but cannot tell where it comes from and where it goes. So is everyone who is born of the Spirit (John 3:6–8).

John tells us that this birth is not primarily dependent on the will of a human being. This birth is 'of God'. If we are going to receive eternal life, God must give it. We are as entirely dependent upon him for eternal life as we were when we were physically born. The apostle Paul makes this clear when writing to Christians. He says:

> And you He made alive, who were dead in trespasses and sins, ... But God, who is rich in mercy, because of His great love with which He loved us, even when we were dead in trespasses, made us alive together with Christ, ... For by grace you have been saved through faith, and that not of yourselves; it is the

> gift of God, not of works, lest anyone should boast' (Ephesians 2:1, 4–5, 8–9).

The picture of someone who is spiritually dead is very powerful to bring home to us that only God can bring new life. It is God who gives the new birth and adopts those who believe. But even their faith is not down to their ancestry, intelligence or lack of it, personality, or any other thing to be found in them. It is God alone who provides everything necessary for this new birth. Paul emphasizes that it is certainly not to do with anything we have done, so no one can boast in themselves. It is a gift which has not been earned.

I have spent well over forty years now preaching the gospel of Christ and I often imagine it is similar to standing in a graveyard calling to all the dead people to come to life. The picture given to us in the Bible is that we are as spiritually dead as those in the graveyard are physically dead. Yet, when Christ and his gospel are preached, although many remain spiritually dead, there are those who incredibly believe. I say 'incredibly' because it is a miracle of the first order. God has done it.

All this may sound completely alien to some. It certainly did to me when I first heard it. But why should it be so strange when we live in a world which demonstrates God giving sunshine and water in its season to bring new life; when we see what was dead now blossoming into new life all around us?

We are taught in the Bible that a person experiencing this new birth is no more of a chance happening than our natural birth. With our natural birth, we may trace all kinds of chance twists and turns to explain who we are and how we appeared from a human perspective. This is also true of a spiritual birth.

The apostle Paul liked relating how he became a Christian and the specific circumstances of his conversion. He spoke about what he used to be like, and what he believed. He told us how he set off to Damascus and what his purposes were in so doing. He told us he was on the road to Damascus when he was converted, and then he tells us the details of his encounter with Christ. Christians today enjoy relating the details of how they became Christians with all its twists and turns. These detailed experiences are interesting and helpful to know. But the apostle Paul traces God's plans right back to before the world was created:

> ... just as He chose us in Him before the foundation of the world, that we should be holy and without blame before Him in love, having predestined us to adoption as sons by Jesus Christ to Himself according to the good pleasure of His will, to the

> praise of the glory of His grace, by which He made us accepted in the Beloved (Ephesians 1:4–6).

Elsewhere we are told, 'Whatever the LORD pleases He does, in heaven and in earth' (Psalm 135:6). When the apostle Paul wants to emphasize how it is God alone who gives new life, he quotes what God said to Moses:

> For He says to Moses, 'I will have mercy on whomever I will have mercy, and I will have compassion on whomever I will have compassion.' So then it is not of him who wills, nor of him who runs, but of God who shows mercy (Romans 9:15–16).

This Bible teaching that God is in complete control of everything, including us and our lives, is not appealing to those who insist human beings are entirely in control of their own destinies.

On one occasion Jesus said:

> 'Therefore I have said to you that no one can come to Me unless it has been granted to him by My Father.' From that time many of His disciples went back and walked with Him no more. Then Jesus said to the twelve, 'Do you also want to go away?' But Simon Peter answered Him, 'Lord to whom shall we go? You have the words of eternal life' (John 6:65–68).

Here was a severe test for the disciples. Jesus' world view and his insistence that God really is God, and not some benign being whose purpose is to help us from time to time, is a shock to the system. Peter's reply suggests he may well have thought about leaving Jesus, when his teaching became difficult to accept. What kept him and the others, however, was the recognition of who he was, and the fact that only he could give eternal life. They stayed on board.

Perhaps one of the reasons human beings at the time of Jesus, and many still today, do not receive Christ is explained in the early chapters of the Bible. In the book of Genesis, we are given the account of how human beings first rebelled against God. The temptation they faced from Satan was, if they did what he said and ignored what God said their 'eyes will be opened, and you will be like God, knowing good and evil' (Genesis 3:5). They chose to believe the lies of the devil and not God.

It seems that, from that time on, we have desired to be as God is, resulting in us exalting ourselves, and attempting to diminish God. The truth according to Jesus and the Bible is that we are dependent upon God for everything in this life, and the next. It is hard for those who want the role of God to swallow.

The human being is presented in Scripture as 'being fearfully and wonderfully made', and every person who believes we were made by God need have no fear of having low self- esteem. Each person is unique and an amazing creation. But we are not God, nor do we have his role. We are responsible to God and will one day be required to answer to him—not him to us.

Yet, knowing we are entirely dependent on God is not to be received as bad news because of who he is. Being in his hands is infinitely better than being left to our own devices because of how he is described: 'The Lord is merciful and gracious, slow to anger, and abounding in mercy' (Psalm 103:8). This is the God who 'is love' and has demonstrated that love through the giving of his Son to die. He it is who is the giver of new life; and he it is who invites us to himself.

WHAT DO WE KNOW ABOUT THIS SPIRITUAL BIRTH?

In the same way as someone who wants to learn about childbirth may study midwifery, so we can look at what Jesus and Scripture tell us about the spiritual birth.

We have seen already it is God the Holy Spirit who gives this life, but the apostle Peter also tells us we have 'been born again, not of corruptible seed but incorruptible, through the word of God which lives and abides forever' (1 Peter 1:23).

In the account in Genesis, each day of creation begins with the same words: 'Then God said ...'. It is followed by a summary of all he created as he spoke the universe into being. Such power is also evident here, where Peter tells us it is the Word of God which causes our spiritual and second birth. The Word of God and the Holy Spirit together is how someone becomes a Christian.

As the apostle Paul puts it, 'It pleased God through the foolishness of the message preached to save those who believe' (1 Corinthians 1:21). He refers to the message, 'through the word of God', as foolishness because that was the opinion of many who did not receive Jesus as the Christ. This remains true to this day, as many think it foolish to trust in the crucifixion of Jesus for the forgiveness of their sins. The apostle Paul insists, however, that 'we preach Christ crucified' (1 Corinthians 1:23), because believing God's gospel is how he brings about the spiritual birth.

The Word of God and the Holy Spirit together is how someone becomes a Christian.

It reminds me of a story I once heard about a church who had erected this text, 'We preach Christ crucified,' on a sign close to a tree outside their church building. The tree grew quickly and eventually hid the last word, so it read, 'We preach Christ.' It was not long before the next word was hidden from view, so passers-by could only see, 'We preach.' No one trimmed the tree so finally, only 'We' was visible.

Perhaps the story acts as a metaphor of what happens in some churches that fail to see how new life in Christ is brought about. Their embarrassment of having a gospel that many think is foolish causes them to let their message slip out of view. It is certainly true that many churches have left the gospel message behind to emphasize the 'we', thinking no one can object to us standing for 'community'. They happily ditch the original message of Jesus; his crucifixion, resurrection, repentance and faith in him are no longer heard.

When however, the Word of God is accompanied by the Holy Spirit, we see God's creative power in the hearts of human beings. Jesus, during his ministry, promised he would send the Holy Spirit after his own departure, and told us what he would do:

> And when He [the Holy Spirit] has come, He will convict the world of sin, and of righteousness, and of judgement' (John 16:8).

The Holy Spirit makes clear what previously had not been understood.

The Holy Spirit makes clear what previously had not been understood. He causes people to see their sin, Christ's righteousness, and the certainty of judgement as realities. It is this new consciousness that gives the evidence God is creating a new creation.

I have heard a number of testimonies which help us understand this. I have a friend who is a doctor and heard her account recently of how she became a Christian. She said she was brought to the point where she believed the message of the gospel was true, but still knew she was not yet a Christian. It was only when the reality of sin, righteousness and judgement were brought home to her that she was brought to repent of her sin and believe in Christ. What had made the difference? According to the teaching of Scripture, she had entered into a new life created by the Holy Spirit who had brought home these truths which she readily embraced. From a spiritual corpse to a living new baby in Christ, the Holy Spirit had been at work convicting her.

A DESCRIPTION OF A NEW CHRISTIAN

What God does in a person is he changes us from the inside out, making us entirely new. As Paul puts it, 'Therefore, if anyone is in Christ, he is a new creation; old things have passed away; behold, all things have become new' (2 Corinthians 5:17).

Perhaps one of the best descriptions of this 'new creation' is found in Matthew, chapter 5, in one of Jesus' most famous sermons. It is called the *Sermon on the Mount* because he was teaching his disciples on a mountain. He begins by describing nine characteristics of those he considers blessed. The word, 'blessed', or 'blest', is used sometimes to simply show appreciation for the circumstances a person finds themselves in. They are happy with their lot.

In Scripture however, the word is used with an eternal perspective. A person is considered blessed when they have been saved, forgiven by God, given eternal life and adopted as his child. This makes them eternally happy. Let's look at those characteristics one by one as described in Matthew chapter 5:

- *'Blessed are the poor in spirit' (v. 3).* Here is a person who knows they are spiritually bankrupt before God. They do not think they are wonderful, worthy people who are better than others, because they have been taught by the Holy Spirit something of their own sin.
- *'Blessed are those who mourn' (v. 4).* Knowing their own rebellion against God they are repentant.
- *'Blessed are the meek' (v. 5).* Having realized they are sinful, they have a changed attitude when it comes to judging others. They no longer think it is other people who are always to blame for everything. A humility enters which affects their relationships.
- *'Blessed are those who hunger and thirst for righteousness' (v. 6).* As the Holy Spirit convinces them of sin, they become aware of their unrighteousness. If they are ever to fulfil what they were originally created for—a relationship with God—they understand it is righteousness they need. We have seen how totally impossible it is for us to fully love God and our neighbour

as we ought, so we cannot earn a righteousness ourselves. But, as this person hungers and thirsts for righteousness, the apostle Paul explains where it can be found:

> Now we know that whatever the law says, it says to those who are under the law, that every mouth may be stopped, and all the world may become guilty before God. Therefore, by the deeds of the law no flesh will be justified in His sight, for by the law is the knowledge of sin. But now the righteousness of God apart from the law is revealed, being witnessed by the Law and the Prophets, even the righteousness of God, through faith in Jesus Christ, to all and on all who believe (Romans 3:19–22).

Faith in Christ, says Paul, is what we need. Relying on keeping God's law will only make us realize how much we have broken it. We will have nothing to say, because we know we are guilty. But for believers, described as the 'blessed', God gives them a righteousness as a gift from himself. This is not dependent on their

Relying on keeping God's law will only make us realize how much we have broken it.

own efforts but is a gift from him which we receive through faith.

- *'Blessed are the merciful' (v. 7).* Once a person begins to understand how much they have been forgiven by God, a new principle is at work within them. If you have been forgiven a debt of ten million pounds, you will find it easier to forgive someone who owes you ten pounds. When we begin to understand how much God has forgiven us, we are more inclined to forgive others.
- *'Blessed are the pure in heart' (v. 8).* It is the heart which has been changed. It is now at war with the many false gods which seek to oust God from his rightful place. The Bible talks about false gods or idols as anything which would take the place of God as the most important thing in our lives. What we live for, what we desire most, becomes our god. The Holy Spirit focuses the heart on Christ above all else.
- *'Blessed are the peacemakers' (v. 9).* The apostle Paul tells us God has made peace with us. He has reconciled us to himself. We are to consider ourselves as ambassadors for Christ to plead with others to also be reconciled:

> Now all things are of God, who has reconciled us to Himself through Jesus Christ, and has

> given us the ministry of reconciliation, that is, that God was in Christ reconciling the world to Himself, not imputing their trespasses to them, and has committed to us the word of reconciliation ... Now then, we are ambassadors for Christ, as though God were pleading through us: we implore you on Christ's behalf, be reconciled to God. For He has made Him who knew no sin to be sin for us, that we might become the righteousness of God in Him (2 Corinthians 5:18–21).

As God has made peace with us, so we desire the end of hostilities, and a new peace between all human beings and God. This means we choose a desire for peace above conflict—peace with God and with each other.

- *'Blessed are those who are persecuted for righteousness' sake' (v. 10).* It is one thing to suffer deservedly for our own wrongdoings, but what about those occasions when a person suffers for what is right and true? They too are blessed in the sight of God.

The last of these descriptions, which follows is more specific:

> 'Blessed are you when they revile and persecute you, and say all kinds of evil against you falsely for

> My sake. Rejoice and be exceedingly glad, for great is your reward in heaven, for so they persecuted the prophets who were before you' (v. 11–12).

Jesus includes a reason why he calls such people blessed after each description. I have included the reason only in the last quote to illustrate how he has eternity in mind. The word, 'blessed', used ordinarily would never include people who are 'poor in spirit, mourn, and are persecuted'. But Jesus' world view always has an eternal perspective.

These, then, are the characteristics of the new creation. It is a description of those who are 'born of God' and therefore, eternally blessed. It is the work of the Holy Spirit and the Word of God. A new life principle is at work.

I have sometimes heard this teaching of Jesus presented as though he is telling us what we ought to be like and for what we should strive: a kind of Christian manifesto of aims for the future, and how his kingdom should look. This does not, however, appear to be chiefly a description of how a Christian ought to be, but how they are now. Jesus is not primarily telling us here what he requires from us, but what he has made of us.

Jesus tells us what he wants from us elsewhere in the Gospels. His consistent message is:

> If anyone desires to come after Me, let him deny himself, and take up his cross, and follow Me. For whoever desires to save his life will lose it, but

> whoever loses his life for My sake will find it. For what profit is it to a man if he gains the whole world, and loses his own soul? (Matthew 16:24–26).

We are not to put ourselves first anymore, but we are to obey Christ and willingly suffer any hardships that come our way as a consequence. We saw how the rich young ruler who came to Jesus wanting eternal life could not change his own desires to put Christ first in his life. But he is not alone. Left to ourselves, who could? But when God changes us from the inside out, and makes us 'poor in spirit', hungering and thirsting after 'righteousness' and prepared to have Christ and eternal life even if it means persecution, the choice becomes easy.

Many people today think that Christianity is a religion where we are told not to do the things we enjoy but replace them by doing religious things. This does not sound very appealing. What such people do not understand is that God gives new desires when he changes us.

I led a meeting today of believers, to study the Bible and pray together. At the beginning of the meeting, I looked around and asked, how many of us would have chosen to spend our afternoon doing this a few years ago? We all laughed, because we could remember when it would have seemed impossible for us to willingly choose to spend our time on a sunny afternoon doing this and actually enjoy it. God had given us new desires.

John tells us elsewhere why it is that a believer in Christ loves God: 'We love Him because He first loved us' (1 John 4:19). When someone recognizes the extent of God's love in giving Christ to die for us, forgiving us, adopting us and granting eternal life, they cannot help but love him. Such a person desires to show their love in return and listen to Jesus when he tells us, 'If you love Me, keep My commandments' (John 14:15). This means 'love' is the chief motive for following the Lord Jesus Christ. Doing what he tells us to do is how we express our love to him. This is very different from those who try to do what God wants, in order to earn a place in heaven.

'Love' is the chief motive for following the Lord Jesus Christ. Doing what he tells us to do is how we express our love to him.

Many religions give rules to follow and claim the faithful will be rewarded in heaven if they are diligent. Christ, however, forgives people the moment they repent and believe. The transformation in the person's life is because of love towards him for all he has already done, not an attempt to earn his blessing.

Recently I preached at a church where we had a time of prayer. It was their custom not to pray silently, but for each one to speak their personal prayers out loud at the same time. They would do so quietly until someone would speak up in prayer and the others would remain silent until they had finished. They would then continue quietly praying audibly.

A prayer I overheard was from a woman rejoicing in the fact that God had saved her. She repeated how wonderful it was and how easy it was to bow the knee to Jesus. She owned him as her Lord and was glad to follow him. One theme she kept coming back to was to thank him because she was amazed how easy it was to put him first and obey him. She related how for years she had wanted forgiveness and eternal life but could never bring herself to deny herself, take up her cross and follow him. Now she could, and she could hardly believe that what had been impossible for years, was now not only possible, but so incredibly easy.

What had happened? The Word of God and the Holy Spirit had been at work in her heart. She had been changed on the inside. It was now her will to have Christ and eternal life above all else. She had been brought to gladly choose Jesus above all else, and he had brought to her the assurance that she was his. She had responded to Jesus' invitation:

> 'Come to Me, all you who labour and are heavy laden, and I will give you rest. Take My yoke upon you and learn from Me, for I am gentle and lowly in heart, and you will find rest for your souls. For

> my yoke is easy and My burden is light' (Matthew 11:28–30).

She was overwhelmed that the burden of obeying Christ was so light.

Jesus ends his *Sermon on the Mount* by relating a memorable story:

> Therefore, whoever hears these sayings of Mine, and does them, I will liken him to a wise man who built his house on the rock (Matthew 7:24).

This story relates to the person who obeys what Christ says as opposed to the person who builds his house upon sand. When the storms of this life with all its troubles blow upon us, the person who obeys Christ remains firm while the person who ignores his teaching is swept away. But to obey his teaching requires an inward change first.

Many people can live their lives without much thought of God. Jesus, and certainly the Bible, are of no interest to them. Yet some hear the message, recognize who Jesus is, receive him by faith, repent of their sin, and follow him. These are the people who have been born again by the Holy Spirit. We do not know who will respond to Jesus' invitation. It is impossible to analyze and predict, because we cannot identify a type of person who may believe in Christ. As we see from Jesus' ministry, he seemed to specialize in saving people who some would consider very unlikely candidates.

It is when the reality of God strikes home, and we see we have broken his commandments that we begin to seek after him. When we understand the gospel and see Jesus has accomplished for us all that is needed, we are given hope. And then, when we are brought to repent and believe in Jesus through the working of the Holy Spirit, we begin our new life.

If you are experiencing such a spiritual change, you can be sure it is because God is at work in your heart. You will love him, and be drawn to choose Christ above all else, because he has chosen and loved you first; you cannot help but choose and love him.

6 Jesus described—His glory, grace and truth

The Gospel of John, chapter 1, verse 14 says:

And the Word became flesh and dwelt among us, and we beheld His glory, the glory as of the only begotten of the Father, full of grace and truth.

Jesus, the Word, 'became flesh'. He who is God took on human nature and lived among human beings on this earth. We have been eyewitnesses to his glory, says John. The glory of the 'only begotten of the Father' refers to the uniqueness of Jesus. He is, as often referred to in Scripture, the Son of God. This does not mean that Scripture teaches he was born and came into being through God as his Father. We have already seen that 'The Word was with God, and the Word was God.' It is rather a reference to him being of the same nature as God the Father and speaks of his relationship and role with him. He alone, because of this unique relationship with the Father, fully reveals to us all that is God.

There are three key words in this verse which describe not only John's experience of the Lord Jesus Christ, but the experience of every believer who through faith begins to get to know Jesus on a day-to-day basis. We shall look in turn at these words to dig deeper into what John is saying about Jesus and the implications for us.

GLORY

Any one of the twelve apostles Jesus had chosen would be able to say they knew him well. They had left their previous occupations to be with him during his ministry. But John, along with Peter and James, seemed particularly close to him as, on a number of occasions, they were chosen to be with him, instead of the full company of disciples. John uses the word, 'glory', to describe the greatness and perfection he saw in Jesus.

The root meaning of 'glory' is to convey the idea of something with substance as opposed to something lightweight. In a world where trivia can often capture our minds, John presents Jesus as someone who is worth considering. It is as if he takes a spotlight to observe all that he is and all he does, so we can see him clearly. This revealing of Jesus is the culmination of how God gently reveals himself and his purposes progressively through the revelation of Scripture.

God's glory can be seen in all manner of things, not least in his creation:

> The heavens declare the glory of God; And the firmament shows His handiwork (Psalm 19:1).

> Holy, holy, holy is the LORD of hosts; The whole earth is full of His glory! (Isaiah 6:3).

Scripture tells us that when human beings first rebelled against God, it affected the whole cosmos and we live our lives on an earth that has now been spoilt from what it was originally. Even so, it is undeniable that we are often in awe of what we call the natural world: the beauty of a sunset; an ocean; the magnificence of a mountain range; and the huge variety of plant life and animals. The human being is presented as the pinnacle of God's creation, which prompted David to say:

> You formed my inward parts; You covered me in my mother's womb. I will praise You, for I am fearfully and wonderfully made (Psalm 139:13–14).

Some of us were brought up in areas where the great sights of this world were well out of reach but, even then, it did not escape our notice how incredible the human being is.

Wherever we live, we have the greatest example of God's glory in creation when we take note of the human being, even with all our defects.

We can learn something of God by observing what he has made. But it has its limitations. It is in the Bible that we learn how God has revealed more of himself to us.

There are incidents in the Old Testament when God

particularly reveals something of his character and purposes to show us His glory.

One such occasion was when God first appeared to Moses as he was caring for a flock of sheep in the desert. Moses saw a bush on fire, yet the bush was not being burned up by the flame. When he went to investigate, God spoke to him. He introduced himself as the God of Abraham, Isaac and Jacob, and told Moses he had been chosen to lead the slave nation of Israel out of their captivity in Egypt. Moses understandably had a lot of questions to ask:

> Then Moses said to God, 'Indeed, when I come to the children of Israel and say to them, "The God of your fathers has sent me to you," and they say to me, "What is His name?" what shall I say to them?' And God said to Moses, 'I AM WHO I AM.' And He said, 'Thus you shall say to the children of Israel, "I AM has sent me to you"' (Exodus 3:13–14).

This is one of a number of occasions when God makes himself known by a miraculous manifestation of his presence, and then speaks, revealing who he is and what are his purposes. By the time the Old Testament has come to its completion, God has revealed to us a great deal about himself, and his purposes for sending his Messiah.

Luke, in his Gospel, then records the announcement by

angels of Christ's birth to shepherds in the fields outside Bethlehem:

> Then the angel said to them, 'Do not be afraid, for behold, I bring you good tidings of great joy which will be to all people. For there is born to you this day in the city of David a Saviour, who is Christ the Lord' (Luke 2:10–11).

God again, at a significant time in the unfolding of his purposes, uses a miraculous manifestation of his presence. In this case, the appearing of spiritual beings—angels—who are a part of his original creation. The announcement is brought to an end with 'a multitude of the heavenly host praising God and saying: "Glory to God in the highest, And on earth peace, goodwill toward men"' (Luke 2:13–14). Little by little our eyes are brought into focus with the gradual revealing of God and his purposes so we can see his glory in his goodness and compassion.

It is worth noting how God reveals what he has to say in everyday situations, so we are not overwhelmed by immediately seeing him in his full glory. When I was a young Christian, I read a few articles by Verna Wright who was Professor of Rheumatology at the University of Leeds, and a medical advisor for the U.K. government. I never met him to speak to personally, but I did have the opportunity to see and hear him on one occasion. He was not speaking in his capacity of being a world expert on rheumatology or teaching his students. Verna was a Christian who believed the Bible was true. So often in the summer he could be found on a beach in the U.K. telling people how they may have eternal life through believing in Jesus Christ.

That is where I saw him, lying flat down on his belly and propping himself up under his chin so he could be eye to eye with a little child, telling them simply about Jesus and his love. I was profoundly moved by the sight. Here was a man who was a giant intellectually and sought out for his learning and expertise in medical matters. Yet, the only time I heard him speak was when I overheard him talking to a five-year-old face to face, using the simplest words and ideas so the child may understand. This, as I understand it, is how God gently passes on his truth to us.

When we are confronted with all that God is, it is all too great to take in. He is presented to us as eternal, unchanging, and infinite, all knowing, everywhere present, and all powerful; the God who had no beginning and will never come to an end; the God who is 'the same yesterday, today and forever' (Hebrews 13:8), never diminishing in his knowledge and power as all things emanate from him. There is no thing or knowledge outside of him because he alone is God. Yet God chooses

When we are confronted with all that God is, it is all too great to take in.

to reveal these things to us in simple terms and ordinary circumstances little by little.

Even then it can all prove too much for us, as it was for Peter, James and John when they had a glimpse of how great Jesus is. Jesus had taken them onto a mountain by themselves where we read:

> He was transfigured before them. His face shone like the sun, and His clothes became as white as the light. ... [They then experienced a bright cloud overshadowing them,] and suddenly a voice came out of the cloud, saying, 'This is My beloved Son, in whom I am well pleased. Hear Him!' And when the disciples heard it, they fell on their faces and were greatly afraid. But Jesus came and touched them and said 'Arise, and do not be afraid' (Matthew 17:2, 5–7).

Here, these three disciples were given a glimpse of the unique glory of God now being revealed in Jesus. God had expressed himself and communicated to us before, but now the full revelation of himself is to be found in Jesus presented to us as the Word. The writer to Hebrews puts it like this:

> God, who at various times and in various ways spoke in time past to the fathers by the prophets, has in these last days spoken to us by His Son, whom He has appointed heir of all things, through

> whom also He made the worlds; who being the brightness of His glory and the express image of His person, and upholding all things by the word of His power, when He had by Himself purged our sins, sat down at the right hand of the Majesty on high (Hebrews 1:1–3).

We see 'the brightness of His glory' in Jesus. But especially as he fulfils the purposes of his Father, by dying on the cross.

As the time came for Christ to die, he prayed:

> 'Father, the hour has come. Glorify Your Son, that Your Son also may glorify You, as You have given Him authority over all flesh, that He should give eternal life to as many as You have given Him. And this is eternal life, that they may know You, the only true God, and Jesus Christ whom You have sent. I have glorified You on the earth. I have finished the work which You have given Me to do. And now, O Father, glorify Me together with Yourself, with the glory which I had with You before the world was' (John 17:1–5).

As Christ drew near to accomplishing his assignment, it was the cross and his resurrection he had clearly in view, praying 'that they also whom You gave Me may be with Me where I am, that they may behold My glory which You have given Me' (John 17:24). God's full glory can be seen as the glory of Jesus Christ dawns upon us: 'For it pleased the Father that in Him all the fullness should dwell' (Colossians 1:19).

It is when Jesus voluntarily presents himself as 'the Lamb of God to take away the sin of the world' (John 1:29) we see his glory at its brightest. We knew he was a good man. His life was used to help others, and his compassion, courage, justice and love shone through in everything he did. But to suffer and die as he did on behalf of others, who were undeserving of such kindness, takes us to a whole new level. It is at the cross we see the climax of all God has to say to us concerning who he is and what he is doing. John tells us he can testify to how great Jesus is, because 'we beheld His glory'. The word, 'glory', is used then, when someone can see and perceive something of the being and purposes of God.

It is at the cross we see the climax of all God has to say to us concerning who he is and what he is doing.

GRACE

John mentions two characteristics of Jesus which show his glory. The first of these is grace. He was full of it. Grace is one of those words that has numerous meanings depending on how it is used. It can describe someone who is courteous or elegant but, in the Bible, it is mainly used to describe God's unfailing love towards us.

When Moses wanted to see something of the glory of God he asked:

> 'Please show me your glory.' Then he [God] said, 'I will make all My goodness pass before you, and I will proclaim the name of the LORD before you. I will be gracious to whom I will be gracious, and I will have compassion on whom I will have compassion' (Exodus 33:18–19).

God responds to Moses' request by revealing his name, goodness and compassion to show Moses his glory. This goes to the heart of how the word, 'grace', is used to describe God's free unmerited favour towards sinful and rebellious humans. We have many examples given to us in Scripture of such grace being seen in Jesus. His whole life shows us what love is really like.

John records an incident where some of the religious leaders brought a woman to Jesus who had committed adultery. Their purpose was to trap him into saying something which would incriminate him, so they challenged him by saying, 'Teacher, this woman was caught in adultery, in the very act. Now Moses, in the law, commanded us that such should be stoned. But what do you say?' (John 8:4–5). How did Jesus respond?

> Jesus stooped down and wrote on the ground with

> His finger as though He did not hear. So when they continued asking Him, He raised Himself up and said to them, 'He who is without sin among you, let him throw a stone at her first.' And again He stooped down and wrote on the ground (John 8:6–8).

These religious leaders who humiliated and condemned the woman did not understand that:

> God did not send His Son into the world to condemn the world, but that the world through Him might be saved. He who believes in Him is not condemned; but he who does not believe is condemned already, because he has not believed in the name of the only begotten Son of God (John 3:17–18).

They brought a sinner to Jesus so he may condemn her. Yet Jesus specifically says he has not come to condemn. It is like going into a baker's shop and asking for a haircut. You will no doubt be told you have come to the wrong person. You need the barber. They had brought the sinner to the wrong person to have her condemned. He had not come to do that. It was not on his agenda.

As a result of Jesus challenging the religious leaders to consider first whether they had ever sinned before throwing the first stone we read:

> Those who heard it, being convicted by their conscience, went out one by one, beginning with the oldest even to the last. And Jesus was left alone,

> and the woman standing in the midst. When Jesus had raised Himself up and saw no one but the woman, He said to her, 'Woman, where are those accusers of yours? Has no one condemned you?' She said, 'No one Lord.' And Jesus said to her, 'Neither do I condemn you; go and sin no more' (John 8:9–11).

Jesus seems to be doing two things here:

- He makes it clear that he did not come to condemn sinners but to save them. This woman was guilty of breaking God's law, but she was forgiven and not condemned because the Lord was full of grace. This is our hope. Jesus was criticized for befriending notoriously bad people, and it did not go down well with the religious leaders. Yet he spent a great deal of his time with people who were considered outcasts in society or immoral, and many of them were changed through their encounter. His grace is seen in his immense compassion for sinners. It is the heart of all he came to do. It is the glorious gospel message which is by far the best news anyone can receive on this earth. For anyone who desires to follow him, and be like him, this is one of his unique characteristics by which we can recognize his disciples from those who are merely religious. He, like his Father, loves sinners. He came to save us.

When the juggernaut of the law confronts us and we have no hope, Christ intervenes with his love and mercy for us and rescues us from destruction.

- When he writes in the sand he is not simply doodling or showing indifference, but it appears to be a reference to something the prophet Jeremiah said:

> All who forsake You shall be ashamed. Those who depart from Me shall be written in the earth, because they have forsaken the LORD, the fountain of living waters (Jeremiah 17:13).

The second point Jesus was making by writing in the sand was that those religious leaders who brought the woman to him in the first place, had in effect forsaken the Lord and abandoned mercy. They had not recognized and received Jesus for who he is, nor believed his gospel. As a result, they were 'ashamed' and 'condemned already, because [they] had not believed in the name of the only begotten Son of God' (John 3:18). Yet this event, along with many other examples show Jesus' willingness and ability to forgive sin.

One other memorable example was when a man who was paralyzed was brought by four of his friends to a house where Jesus was teaching:

> When Jesus saw their faith, He said to the paralytic, 'Son your sins are forgiven you.' And some of the scribes were sitting there and reasoning in their hearts, 'Why does this man speak blasphemies like this? Who can forgive sins but God alone?' (Mark 2:5–7).

This disabled man was clearly brought to Jesus because they all believed he could heal him.

Jesus, however, addressed a need which was even more important. He announced he was forgiven of his sins. We can understand the scribes, who were considered the expert interpreters of the Old Testament, when they questioned Jesus' ability to forgive this man his sin.

We have seen that ultimately all sin is against God himself, so God alone can forgive sin. That is true enough. It would be a futile gesture if someone who had not been sinned against announced forgiveness to the one guilty of sin. But the scribes had not recognized nor received Jesus as the Christ; that is why they considered his announcement as blasphemy.

Jesus, though, was willing to produce evidence that it was within his authority to forgive sin. He said to them:

> 'Which is easier, to say to the paralytic, "Your sins are forgiven you," or to say, "Arise take up your bed and walk"? But that you may know that the Son of Man has power on earth to forgive sins'—He said

> to the paralytic, 'I say to you, arise, take up your bed, and go to your house.' Immediately he arose, took up the bed, and went out in the presence of them all, so that all were amazed and glorified God, saying, 'We never saw anything like this!' (Mark 2:9–12).

Jesus' compassion extended to not only healing his body but also forgiving his sin. Many witnessed his grace and were 'amazed'.

As we would now expect, the light of Jesus' grace is seen brightest at the cross. When Jesus was being crucified, he looked out onto the mocking faces of those who jeered and threw insults at him and prayed, 'Father, forgive them, for they do not know what they do' (Luke 23:34). Astonishing. We have here a cameo of what Jesus was achieving as the Lamb of God in dealing with sin once and for all.

Literally millions of people in the ages to come would be brought to believe in this man and, through faith, be forgiven. But here was a specific prayer for those responsible for his suffering. The prayer was answered in a matter of weeks, as we have already seen, on the day of Pentecost, when many who had been responsible for his death were brought to realize what they had done. They repented and were baptized and joined together to form the first Christian church.

Jesus was crucified with two criminals suffering the

same death at either side of him. Originally both criminals were joining in with those in the crowd who were insulting him. But one of them had a change of heart and acknowledged Jesus had done nothing wrong, even asking him:

'Lord, remember me when You come into Your kingdom.' And Jesus said to him, 'Assuredly, I say to you, today you will be with Me in Paradise' (Luke 23:42–43).

This man was assured that he would have life—eternal life—in paradise with Jesus.

I have spoken to a number of people over the years about *grace*, and sometimes heard the response that it does not seem fair. For someone to live a life which harms many and then, at the last moment, to believe in Jesus and receive his grace does not seem fair; especially if others, who have not done such bad things, are still answerable for their sins. I am always encouraged when I hear someone respond in that way, because it shows they have understood something about grace. Grace is not about fairness. It is the sheer unmitigated mercy from God, who is love, towards an undeserving sinner. That is why this gospel is relevant to everybody. And that is why Jesus is 'full of grace'.

Grace is not about fairness. It is the sheer unmitigated mercy from God, who is love, towards an undeserving sinner.

I have also met people who understand how God saves undeserving sinners even in the last moments of their life and find a false comfort in that. They, like the rich young ruler, desire eternal life but find it impossible to repent of their particular idol and god, but they vainly hope that, once they are near death, they can simply say sorry and have what they consider the best of this life and then the next.

The criminal crucified with Jesus was most certainly saved from the consequences of his sin as far as eternity is concerned. But I remember reading an experienced pastor saying, 'There are very few death-bed repentances.' My first question was, 'How could he possibly know?' The next few sentences anticipated my question. He lived at a time when it was not always clear when someone was facing death or about to recover, but they feared they would die. It was his observation that he had spoken to many who thought they were about to die and said they were now believing in Jesus but then recovered. On their recovery, they went back to their unbelief and lived their lives completely detached from anything God has ever said.

In other words, they were scratching about for some comfort when they thought they were dying. They believed repentance was an easy option of just saying sorry. But we have already seen it requires a change of heart to leave our idols and believe in Jesus.

I have also heard a number of atheists who have testified that, when it was more likely for them to die than live, they 'did not resort to prayer'. They were proud of their consistency, but I always felt deeply saddened that they continued to refuse God's offer of grace to the last.

The examples of Christ showing the grace of God are evident today. I have known people who would be categorized as the 'worst of sinners' and the 'monsters' of our society, being given eternal life, forgiveness, and being made new creations in Christ. I spent many years visiting a top security prison where there were murderers and men serving life sentences. I have seen some feign a conversion to faith in the hope it will enable an earlier release. But I have also witnessed genuine conversions where men have changed and been made new creations in Christ. I know of terrorists, guilty of hatred and murder, turned around to bring great blessing to many people for the rest of their lives.

I do not speak theoretically about the power of the gospel. John speaks of Jesus, 'full of grace', as an eyewitness of Jesus' life. I cannot do that, but I can testify the gospel of Christ 'is the power of God to salvation for everyone who believes' (Romans 1:16). I have seen that with my own eyes and experienced it.

TRUTH

The second characteristic John mentions which shows the

glory of Jesus is that he was full of truth. When I first began to enquire about God, it was the truth I wanted to know above everything else. That has remained the case to this day. What is fact and reality?—that was my concern and if you have read this far in a book about God and the Bible, I assume it is of importance to you as well. I have often heard the expression, 'if it is true for you', which thinks of truth as relative and dependent on how we respond to something, as to whether it is true or not. So, someone can believe in God and that is seen as true for them, but someone else who does not believe is also seen as holding to the truth as they see it. We, however, are concerned with rock-bottom reality. What is ultimate truth, whether anyone believes it or not?

The question asked by Pontius Pilate, who was ultimately the man in charge at Jesus' crucifixion, remains relevant for today. When Jesus said to Pilate:

> 'You say rightly that I am a king. For this cause I was born, and for this cause I have come into the world, that I should bear witness to the truth. Everyone who is of the truth hears My voice.' Pilate said to Him, 'What is truth?' (John 18:37–38).

Pilate's question appears cynical as he has no intention of hearing any reply but quickly turns away and leaves. Perhaps like many today, he thought there could be no answer or maybe he was afraid of one. Either way, he never waited for a reply. If he had, Jesus may have repeated what he had taught previously:

> 'I am the way, the truth, and the life. No one comes to the Father except through Me' (John 14:6).

Jesus' own view is that he is truth personified. He had told Pilate he was the king of a kingdom which was not of this world, meaning he would reign in the hearts of his subjects until the new kingdom was brought into its completeness at the end of this present world. It was to be a kingdom of truth, as opposed to this world with its abundance of lies, and it was to begin now in the hearts of those who own him as their King.

This claim by Jesus that he was truth personified was borne out by his lifestyle. He had claimed that he perfectly reflects all that is God. This includes a description of God that says, 'It is impossible for God to lie' (Hebrews 6:18). We are told God cannot lie in the context of us being able to fully trust all his promises to us. This is why a believer in Christ can be confident they have eternal life now, even though they are this side of death. As it is explained elsewhere, '... in hope of eternal life which God, who cannot lie, promised before time began' (Titus 1:2).

Like all the claims of Jesus, we see there is a consistency with his life. He is presented to us as uniquely the one without sin, and his insistence on living and telling the truth shines through. This applies to him courageously confronting the religious leaders of the day and speaking the truth to them, even though they had the power and the increasing inclination to have him put to death. As recorded in the Gospel of Matthew, he repeatedly tells them they are hypocrites. He describes them as being:

> '... like whitewashed tombs which indeed appear beautiful outwardly, but inside are full of dead men's bones and all uncleanness. Even so you also outwardly appear righteous to men, but inside you are full of hypocrisy and lawlessness (Matthew 23:27–28).

This was no subtle hint as to what he thought of the religious leaders. For Jesus, it was the truth, so he had to speak it clearly. He did so in full knowledge of the consequences.

In all Jesus does and says, there are no inconsistencies.

We see, then, in all Jesus does and says, there are no inconsistencies. As it is with his Father, so it is with him: 'God is light and in Him is no darkness at all' (1 John 1:5).

On one occasion when speaking to some religious leaders who would not accept what he was saying as true, Jesus told them:

> Because I tell the truth, you do not believe Me. Which of you convicts Me of sin? And if I tell the truth, why do you not believe Me? He who is of

> God hears God's words; therefore, you do not hear, because you are not of God (John 8:45–47).

Yet, because Jesus is full of grace as well as truth, he was able to say elsewhere:

> If anyone hears My words and does not believe, I do not judge him: for I did not come to judge the world but to save the world. He who rejects Me, and does not receive My words, has that which judges him—the word that I have spoken will judge him in the last day. For I have not spoken on My own authority; but the Father who sent Me gave Me a command, what I should say and what I should speak. And I know that His command is everlasting life (John 12:47–50).

Jesus insisted he was truth personified and, therefore, told the truth because the words he spoke were from the Father. They had been given on the Father's authority.

Jesus, truth and Scripture

Jesus' teaching on what truth is extends to his view of Scripture. We have noted already how Jesus consistently used Scripture as the foundation of all he had to say. As we read through the Gospels, we see him obeying Scripture, and the whole direction of his life was with an understanding that he was fulfilling what had been written. As far as he was concerned, the Scriptures were true.

We remember how he referred to his miracles as

evidence of who he was, but he teaches us that Scripture is even more powerful in its evidence than a miracle. When telling of two men who had died, Jesus speaks of one man who was tormented in Hades, while the other was in the comfort of Abraham. The man in torment had five brothers still alive, and he asked Abraham to send the other man back to warn his brothers before they died:

> Abraham said to him, 'They have Moses and the prophets; let them hear them.' And he said, 'No, father Abraham; but if one goes to them from the dead, they will repent.' But he said to him, 'If they do not hear Moses and the prophets, neither will they be persuaded though one rise from the dead' (Luke 16:29–31).

Scripture has been given for us to know the truth. If that is rejected, nothing else will convince us.

Scripture, says Jesus, has been given for us to know the truth. If that is rejected, nothing else will convince us.

Even after his resurrection, when he was physically present with two disciples walking with them on the road to Emmaus, he brought the proof of his resurrection from Scripture.

These disciples had doubted the reports they had heard concerning him coming back to life and, before they recognized who he was, Jesus said, 'O foolish ones, and slow of heart to believe in all that the prophets have spoken!' (Luke 24:25). He rebuked them for not believing the Old Testament prophets who had spoken of the reality of the Messiah overcoming death.

The apostles take the same view as Jesus. Peter tells us:

> For we did not follow cunningly devised fables when we made known to you the power and coming of our Lord Jesus Christ, but were eyewitnesses of His majesty (2 Peter 1:16).

As we have seen, Peter was one of the three apostles who saw Jesus transfigured before them on the mountain. But he goes on to say that Scripture is even greater evidence than what he had personally experienced: 'For prophecy never came by the will of man, but holy men of God spoke as they were moved by the Holy Spirit' (2 Peter 1:21).

Finding truth today can be like trying to grasp a slippery eel. When we access news outlets, we often learn more about our sources' agenda than we do about what is actually true.

Everything is coloured by a belief system: the editorial choosing of what to report, the presentation, and the questions asked are never neutral, as is often claimed. The Lord Jesus Christ and the Bible are not neutral either. But they never claim to be.

I think John speaks for the rest of the Bible as well as himself when he explains where he is coming from.

As we have previously seen, he wrote his Gospel so 'that you may believe that Jesus is the Christ, the Son of God, and that believing you may have life in His name' (John 20:31). He tells us upfront, with no hidden agenda. How refreshing!

The question is however, 'Is what he says manipulative, insincere, false and a pack of lies or true? Is he using exaggeration and lies to promote what he considers the greater good, as many others do?'

I remember a good friend of mine, who I had spoken to about Jesus and the gospel, but he had never really believed it. He lived a very difficult life and sometimes phoned me at different times of the day or night, when he needed help—this was in the days before mobile phones, and so every town had a number of 'phone boxes' provided for the public.

He called me once from a phone box in our local town. I heard my phone ringing but by the time I had answered it he had rung off—this was some time ago before our modern technology, but our telephone provider had just recently introduced a number to phone if you wanted to get straight back to the call you had missed. I phoned the number. I still smile now when I picture my friend gathering his bags of food and cans of beer as he curses me for not answering his call.

Before he got out of the phone box, my returned call arrived. The phone rang. Why is the telephone ringing in a public telephone box? This must be a classic wrong number call. However, he couldn't resist but pick up the phone. I, of course, had no idea who had phoned me, or that it was from a call box. So, when a voice said, 'Hello,' I replied, 'Hello, Mick here.' I was greeted by a very loud scream! My friend had no idea of the new technology, and assumed my totally random call to a phone box was a miraculous act of God. Was that an opportunity to manipulate the truth? I had no doubt it was a providence of God. But miraculous?—not really. Should I go along with his misconception?

There was no choice. Christ is 'truth'. He is truth, personified; he lived it and spoke it. How then, can we manipulate truth to encourage people to believe in him, when it contradicts the essence of the glory of Jesus, and who he is? I could not pretend this was a miracle and he must believe at once because of it, any more than John could. An explanation to him of the new technology brought him from his frenzied dread to a settled state.

There are many who do of course manipulate the truth for their own purposes. We can spot them easily enough as we hear what they have to say and compare it with Scripture, even if many of them accumulate great wealth as a consequence. But could John do that in his Gospel? Could he present Christ as he does, with his emphasis on truth, while wickedly lying in all he writes?

I am conscious that human beings are capable of massive inconsistencies because the core characteristic of the human heart is 'deceitful above all things' (Jeremiah 17:9). But John was chosen by Christ, and he made it known that only one of his original twelve disciples was to prove himself a hypocrite. Jesus had once said:

> 'Did I not choose you, the twelve, and one of you is a devil?' He spoke of Judas Iscariot, the son of Simon, for it was he who would betray Him, being one of the twelve' (John 6:70–71).

Jesus was aware of what would happen before the event. But he indirectly tells us here that the other eleven disciples were not like Judas.

It is easily demonstrated that Christ himself believed the Old Testament and gave his apostles the task of passing on the truth of the gospel. Christians believe Scripture because they follow the example of their Lord, and believe he came back from the dead. There are, of course, many views of the Bible but Christians would choose to believe the man who came back from the dead. That seems a better qualification than a master's degree in theology.

The famous John Wesley, who founded the Methodist Church in the 18th century, reasoned like this:

> The Bible must be the invention either of good men or angels, bad men or devils, or of God. It could not

> be the invention of good men or angels, for they neither would nor could make a book and tell lies all the time they were writing it, saying 'thus says the Lord' when it was their own invention. It could not be the invention of bad men or devils, for they could not make a book that commands all duty, forbids all sin, and condemns their souls to hell for all eternity. Therefore, the Bible must be given by divine inspiration.[1]

Wesley's conclusion that the Bible is ultimately from God is claimed repeatedly in the Old Testament which Jesus knew to be true. Expressions like, 'the LORD spoke', 'the LORD said', and 'the LORD commanded', are scattered throughout, leaving no doubt what they were claiming. The New Testament, likewise, claimed 'All Scripture is given by inspiration of God' (2 Timothy 3:16). God gave Jesus as the Word and breathed out his written word in Scripture. That is why Jesus and Scripture are inseparable. Christians do not worship the written word of Scripture, but worship the living Word, Jesus Christ, who lived his life in harmony with the written word.

God gave Jesus as the Word and breathed out his written word in Scripture. That is why Jesus and Scripture are inseparable.

John and the rest of the Bible present Jesus as truth,

personified. And because of that, truth is vital. He could not have manipulated the truth for what he considered the greater good. John, as an eyewitness, simply states what he has seen with his own eyes: 'We beheld His glory, the glory as of the only begotten of the Father, full of grace and truth' (John 1:14).

Jesus, truth and freedom

When considering the subject of truth, we discover that Jesus relates it to another subject dear to the hearts of modern-day people: that of *freedom*.

It is John who records what Jesus said to some who had believed in Christ:

> 'If you abide in My word, you are My disciples indeed. And you shall know the truth, and the truth shall make you free.' They answered Him, 'We are Abraham's descendants, and have never been in bondage to anyone. How can you say, "You will be made free?"' Jesus answered them, 'Most assuredly, I say to you, whoever commits sin is a slave of sin. And a slave does not abide in the house forever, but a son abides forever. Therefore if the Son makes you free, you shall be free indeed' (John 8:31–36).

These people had initially believed what Jesus was saying. But Christ knew their hearts and told them they must live out the word he was speaking to them as evidence they truly believed. By the end of the conversation, they did not follow him but instead tried to kill him. In the meantime, we have Jesus' view of what real freedom is and how it is related to truth.

'*Freedom*' is a massive question for today, whether it is freedom of speech, political freedom, freedom of education, or a multitude of freedoms considered as human rights. Jesus, here, is saying that ultimate freedom is being freed from slavery to sin through knowing the truth and abiding in it. The Bible tells us we are not what we should be because, ultimately, we are slaves to sin. We simply obey our master at every prompting, and we feel compelled to do what our master says. Our master, however, is sin: the desire to transgress God's law. According to Jesus, this is our predicament and imprisonment. This above all else is what we need to be freed from.

The gospel remains the most relevant and wonderful message for us today.

The woman praying in church, who I mentioned in the last chapter, was in effect thanking God for the freedom she had found. She was no longer a slave to sin, but now free to enjoy her new relationship with God. She had a new master who was Christ, to whom she gladly bowed the knee. The truth had set her free. The gospel remains the most relevant and wonderful message for us today.

Notes

1 Blanchard, John, *Right with God*, (Edinburgh: Banner of Truth Trust, 1971), p. 10.

7 God's big plan

The Gospel of John, chapter 1, verses 15 to 17 says:

John bore witness of Him and cried out, saying, 'This was He of whom I said, "He who comes after me is preferred before me, for He was before me."'
And of His fullness we have all received, and grace for grace.
For the law was given through Moses, but grace and truth came through Jesus Christ.

John, the Gospel writer, now takes us back to the testimony of John the Baptist. We have seen how John the Baptist described Jesus as 'The Lamb of God who takes away the sin of the world' (John 1:29), referring to how Christ would accomplish his assignment. Now we hear him saying he is 'preferred before me'. John was keen to point out that, just because he began to preach before Jesus, it did not mean he should be thought of more highly than him. Christ surpassed him and ranked above him in every way, not least in that he came before John in the sense that he is eternal.

This was not a disappointment for John. A few verses on in John's Gospel, when John the Baptist was asked who he was, he quotes the Old Testament prophet Isaiah to explain:

> I am the voice of one crying in the wilderness: 'make straight the way of the LORD' (John 1:23).

He understood his role perfectly. He was, in effect, a signpost to point people away from himself to Christ. When comparing himself with Jesus, he said, 'He who is coming after me is mightier than I, whose sandals I am not worthy to carry' (Matthew 3:11).

Later on, when the ministries of John the Baptist and Jesus overlapped, it was pointed out to John that Jesus' disciples were baptizing more than him. Maybe they were expecting John to be disappointed with the news, but instead he was delighted, saying:

> He must increase, but I must decrease. He who comes from heaven is above all (John 3:30–31).

John, the Gospel writer, also brings us back to considering Jesus in his next verses. Having told us Christ was full of grace and truth, he now tells us these have overflowed to us. We have received 'grace for grace' or 'grace upon grace' in great abundance.

The law, we are told, was given through Moses, and is a blessing to us as the vital foundation in God's overall plan. But we are glad the giving of the law was not the final revelation from God, otherwise we would be left to face a certain condemnation because we are all law breakers. Grace and truth came through Jesus, and John specifically focuses here on grace. The free, unmerited favour of God flows from Christ with innumerable blessings. 'Grace for grace' is not telling us one grace replaces another. But it does suggest a continual pouring out of blessing, in line with how Scripture sheds increasing light as more is revealed.

THE BLESSINGS OF GRACE

Let's use an illustration to help us understand what this phrase, 'grace upon grace', means. Imagine a mountainous landscape. You are surrounded by rocky crags, as you live in the valley. There is one thing you lack which is essential for life: it is water. But, unknown to you, someone is aware of your hopeless situation and they plan to provide for you. They are the source of providing water which flows for miles through the mountain range, mostly underground, but occasionally bursting out onto the surface before disappearing again. As it enters your valley, it again emerges into daylight in full strength as a mighty torrent of water explodes into several tributaries, winding their way through the valley.

Your thirst for water is now met. But more than that, you can now plant and grow what you need to live. You welcomed the water because it quenched your thirst. But now you realize the blessing it brings is that you can grow crops: with strength from food, you can build houses; with hope and a future, you can raise a family; plan for your future and organize; have time to think, invent, create, and live life to the full. The benefits keep coming one after the other. That is the point.

What God has done is to see our dilemma and because of his kindness, mercy and compassion, he has provided all that we need. 'He is love.' We see him expressing his love. He is the source; he provides the water. The Holy Spirit in Scripture is often described in terms of life giving water. He emanates from the source. But also emanating from the source is the spring from which the water bursts into the valley. That is the picture of Christ in our illustration. He is our focus because we can see where the life-giving water comes from. It is to him we go because there we receive gracc. It is from this grace, we receive blessing after blessing. One after another. They just keep coming and coming. It is 'grace upon grace'.

The apostle Paul begins his letter to the church in Ephesus by saying:

> Blessed be the God and Father of our Lord Jesus Christ, who has blessed us with every spiritual blessing in the heavenly places in Christ (Ephesians 1:3).

He is telling us that those who are connected to Jesus through faith are united to him in such a way that every eternal blessing God has to give is now theirs.

If someone is interested in board games, they will have some in their house. The other day I saw a 'Games Compendium' with 100 favourite games in one box. That is a lot of games but even then, someone will notice one of their favourites was not included.

What Paul is saying is that every eternal blessing which comes from God is found in Jesus. When we believe in him, we do not receive one, or a few blessings, but the complete 'blessing compendium'. Not one is missing, and there are no individual blessings to be found outside of him. The source is God, found in Jesus, distributed by the Holy Spirit. God's grace is poured out in his blessings, one after the other, 'grace upon grace'.

We all benefit from God's kindness and receive all manner of blessings from him. Jesus tells us, 'He makes His sun rise on the evil and on the good, and sends rain on the just and on the unjust' (Matthew 5:45). These are blessings from God upon all people. But we are focusing on the eternal blessings which are received through faith in Christ for all who receive him.

We have touched upon a few of the most important of these as we have journeyed through this book together. The gift of God's Son, Jesus, given by the Father is the greatest of all the blessings he gives because every other blessing is found in him. So, when we believe in him, we find that we are declared 'justified' in God's sight. This legal term brings us straight to the courtroom of judgement day, where we learn from the apostle Paul:

> There is therefore now no condemnation to those

> who are in Christ Jesus, who do not walk according to the flesh, but according to the Spirit (Romans 8:1).

From guilty to innocent because of Christ and his death. From condemned to justified. We find forgiveness.

Then, we have seen the courtroom language transformed into the language of family. We learn we have been adopted by God and we become his children, as he frees us from being slaves to sin. Not only are we told we have an eternal home with him, but he takes up residence with us, as the Holy Spirit is given to every believer. It is he who convicted us of our sin and brought us to repentance and new life, but he does not leave once he has accomplished that work. He dwells within us, increasingly revealing more of Christ to us. He is the source of our new life and causes us to grow in our desire to be more like Jesus.

The Bible gives the picture of how trees produce fruit so we can see clearly what type of tree it is. In the same way, the apostle Paul tells us some of the fruit, or characteristics, we displayed without the Holy Spirit. These include such things as adultery, hatred, selfish ambitions, heresies, and drunkenness (Galatians 5:19–21). By way of comparison, he then tells us:

> But the fruit of the Spirit is love, joy, peace, longsuffering, kindness, goodness, faithfulness,

> gentleness, self-control. Against such there is no law (Galatians 5:22–23).

It is his continuing work to make us more like Christ, and who wouldn't desire those qualities?

There are many people who view Christianity as a miserable, guilt-ridden life. My experience, along with countless others, is the exact opposite. Now freed from guilt, we find, from small beginnings, a growing and flourishing of love, joy and peace in our hearts.

What was a miserable time, in my experience, was the period when I had come to believe the gospel was true but continued my sinful lifestyle. Previous to that, with no thought of God, I was able, as the book of Hebrews expresses it, 'to enjoy the passing pleasures of sin' (Hebrews 11:25). Those pleasures do however pass very quickly, as the consequences of a sinful life take root.

Once God begins to make himself known there is a growing dissatisfaction with a life characterized by sin. The resulting sorrow can, according to Scripture, lead to only one of two possible destinations:

> For godly sorrow produces repentance leading to salvation, not to be regretted; but the sorrow of the world produces death (2 Corinthians 7:10).

The godly sorrow leads to repentance which brings us to the joy of salvation. We learn it is God's intention to increasingly bring joy to our hearts.

There was an occasion in the Old Testament where people had gathered to hear the Scriptures read and explained. As they heard all that God had said, they wept together. Their leader, Nehemiah, encouraged them to go and enjoy something to eat, with the explanation: 'Do not sorrow, for the joy of the LORD is your strength' (Nehemiah 8:10). God's intention is not to have us in miserable subjection to him, but to free us by giving an abundance of life with joy.

God's intention is not to have us in miserable subjection to him, but to free us by giving an abundance of life with joy.

This does not mean, however, that when someone becomes a Christian they become perfect or without problems overnight. That simply does not happen for a number of reasons:

First of all, although they have been freed as slaves to sin, they are still sinners. The desire to rebel against God still remains and temptation comes in many different forms. Also, it is possible to quench or resist the Holy Spirit who is working to make us more like Christ. It is not always a painless process as he weans us from old ways of thinking into a new lifestyle. Yet, we are always reliant on the Holy Spirit. The reality of the Christian life is that it is miraculous from start to finish. It is impossible to follow Christ without him.

When the apostle Paul is giving us directions of how the believer should live, he says:

> Let nothing be done through selfish ambition or conceit, but in lowliness of mind let each esteem others better than himself (Philippians 2:3).

To think of everyone else as better than yourself seems an impossible task until we experience the Holy Spirit revealing something of the corruption of our own heart to ourselves. We can only see the outward actions and words of others. Their heart remains hidden to us, but ours isn't, so we see the tip of the iceberg of their sin, but we have revealed to us something of the hidden depths and extent of our own sin. Suddenly the directive Paul gives becomes entirely possible.

This is why the apostle Paul, after saying that believers are no longer slaves to sin, goes on shortly afterwards to point out that, even though his inner self wants to obey God, the old sinful nature is still present with him. His observation is:

> For I know that in me (that is, in my flesh) nothing good dwells; for to will is present with me, but how to perform what is good I do not find (Romans 7:18).

Believers in Christ are not the finished article, but we are a work in progress with each one of us at a different stage on the journey with the Holy Spirit in charge. No wonder Paul was able to say:

> This is a faithful saying and worthy of all acceptance, that Christ Jesus came into the world to save sinners, of whom I am chief (1 Timothy 1:15).

When Paul described himself as the 'chief of sinners', no doubt he had in mind his murderous persecution of Christians before his conversion. But he also makes it clear that after his conversion he is far from perfect. It is interesting that Christ chose the apostle Paul rather than angels to go and spread the message of God's grace. The fact that he was the worst of sinners seems to be his main qualification, as he understood more than the angels of God's grace through his experience of forgiveness. Anyone presenting themselves as better than others have simply not understood Christ's teaching.

Years ago, I had a close friend who was much older than me. He told me of a meeting he had gone to when he was young. It was a Christian event in the inner city where the homeless were invited to a Christmas meal and then followed by a short talk from an invited speaker. He told of the occasion the speaker began his message by saying something like, 'I used to be like you lot: smelly, disgusting layabouts who beg for money. But I'm going to tell you how you can make a success of yourselves like me.' My friend said he didn't hear anymore as he left thinking,

'I'm sure I would have liked him a lot more if he'd stayed the way he was.'

We remember the characteristics of the blessed person: poor in spirit, mourning over their sin, with a hunger and thirst for righteousness. This does not fit well with those who want to present themselves as the paragon to what we are to aspire. We are thankful Christ shows a special care to those with great needs, but we are all included when he says, 'Christ Jesus came into the world to save sinners.'

Having the Holy Spirit is a great blessing for a Christian, yet his work is not yet complete. The struggle between good and evil continues. But for those with faith, it is now in the context of being free and the adopted children of God. Our heavenly Father has proved his love to us and continues to show his forgiveness and patience on a daily basis. When someone becomes a Christian, they remain in total reliance on God's grace day by day until the day they die. God's grace remains their only hope. Justification, forgiveness, adoption, new birth and the Holy Spirit poured out are a few of the blessings here and now of God's grace.

I have spoken to some people who have said that even after 2,000 years of Christ's teaching, the world is still in a mess. Does that mean it hasn't worked? There is a strong case for arguing that where Jesus' teaching has been widely believed and implemented, it has brought great improvements to society. With love at the centre of his message, and an emphasis on care and compassion for each other, it has to make a difference.

Undoubtedly there are many examples of his message being perverted, as it was when he was here on earth. The religious leaders were the main enemies of Jesus then, and often religious leaders now take their place alongside numerous other ideologies, political movements, and tyrants who have made the world worse through their activism.

In his *Sermon on the Mount* in Matthew's Gospel, Jesus describes his disciples as 'the salt of the earth' and 'the light of the world' (Matthew 5:13, 14), so he clearly expects them to make a difference for good. But we remember what he said to Pontius Pilate, that his kingdom was not of this world. It was not on his agenda to lead a rebellion to free his nation from Roman rule. Jesus had an eternal perspective in everything he did. The gospel message is given for sinners to repent of their sin and own him as the 'King of kings and the Lord of lords' (Revelation 19:16). Believers consider Jesus their King now and in obeying him should, and do, make a difference. But he gave no instruction to his disciples for a political uprising, because his plan culminates not on this earth but in a new earth. This brings us to God's big plan and 'the blessings of grace in eternity'.

THE BLESSINGS OF GRACE IN ETERNITY

There is much speculation on the future of our planet. Everyone agrees it is destined to end at some time. The more optimistic predict there is a long time yet. Jesus, however, is recorded as saying on three occasions right at the end of the Bible, 'Behold, I am coming quickly' (Revelation 22:7, 12 and 20). This has the effect of focusing our minds on what is in the future. Jesus has a great deal to say about future events. In all his teaching on this subject it is within the framework of God's overall plan. He is not simply predicting random events, but outlining how God will fulfil all his purposes. We have some of his teaching on this in the Gospel of Matthew, chapters 24 and 25.

He begins by speaking of the near future and the destruction of the temple in Jerusalem, which came about in AD 70. But he then speaks of his coming to the earth again—which coincides with the end of this world—immediately followed by the last judgement.

For Jesus, the end of this world is not the end of all things. As we shall see, it is a glorious beginning.

For people who spend a great deal of time speculating how the world will come to an end, it is important to them because they see it as the end of all things. Jesus agrees this world will end, but he presents it to us in the context of something even more important. The Lord Jesus Christ will return. This is because, for Jesus, the end of this world is not the end of all things. As we shall see, it is a glorious beginning. It is worth remembering at this point that Christians believe what Jesus says because he came back from the dead.

In Matthew 24, Jesus speaks in general terms of what the world must first endure, including wars, famines and earthquakes. He then outlines the specific signs and indications of his return by saying:

> Many false prophets will rise up and deceive many. And because lawlessness will abound, the love of many will grow cold. But he who endures to the end shall be saved. And this gospel of the kingdom will be preached in all the world as a witness to all the nations, and then the end will come (Matthew 24:11–14).

The apostle Peter warns us there will be numerous people who will mock and ridicule this teaching of Jesus. He says:

> ... that scoffers will come in the last days, walking according to their own lusts and saying, 'Where is the promise of his coming? For since the fathers fell asleep, all things continue as they were from the beginning of creation' (2 Peter 3:3–4).

Peter goes on to say:

> The Lord is not slack concerning His promise, as

> some count slackness, but is longsuffering toward us, not willing that any should perish but that all should come to repentance.
>
> But the day of the Lord will come as a thief in the night, in which the heavens will pass away with a great noise, and the elements will melt with fervent heat; both the earth and the works that are in it will be burned up. Therefore, since all these things will be dissolved, what manner of persons ought you to be in holy conduct and godliness, looking for and hastening the coming of the day of God, because of which the heavens will be dissolved, being on fire, and the elements will melt with fervent heat? Nevertheless we, according to His promise, look for new heavens and a new earth in which righteousness dwells. (2 Peter 3:9–13).

Christ clearly teaches that the end of this world is not the end of all things. His view is that there is another world to come where sin does not enslave, lies are not lived, and death is no more. John expresses it like this:

There is another world to come where sin does not enslave, lies are not lived, and death is no more.

> And I heard a loud voice from heaven saying, 'Behold the tabernacle of God is with

> men, and He will dwell with them, and they shall be His people. God Himself will be with them, and be their God. And God will wipe away every tear from their eyes; there shall be no more death, nor sorrow, nor crying. There shall be no more pain, for the former things have passed away.'
> Then He who sat on the throne said, 'Behold I make all things new.' And He said to me, 'Write, for these words are true and faithful' (Revelation 21:3–5).

Notice it is a new heaven and earth created for human beings where God himself shall live.

We see the word, 'heaven', used to describe different things in Scripture. It can mean simply the horizon, as far as we can see with our eyes. It can also be used to describe our universe and beyond: the sun, moon, stars and galaxies which we are still discovering.

But Paul speaks about being caught up into the 'third heaven': 'he was caught up into Paradise and heard inexpressible words, which it is not lawful for a man to utter' (2 Corinthians 12:2–4). This is clearly another dimension altogether. This is the dwelling place of God, where no probe or space exploration can venture. God, and where he lives, is literally out of our orbit, and outside our space and time. All, says the Scriptures, shall be made new—not only new heavens, but a new earth.

When I was a young Christian, I heard heaven described

as 'entirely other'. I don't doubt that is a helpful phrase for those trained in philosophy. But I am not. It is no good to me because I think in pictures and I like to read Scripture and then think about what it means. I'm afraid my brain is not equipped to make any sense of 'entirely other'. Thankfully God crouches down and props his head up so he is face to face with us to explain simply, and in pictures, so we can understand.

You and I know something about this earth; we live on it. Heaven is sometimes thought of in a very vague way—of us joining angels on clouds, as they play harps. No wonder many have been put off by the prospect. Heaven is not described like that at all in the Bible. But it is described as a new earth. The difference from our earth now is that the new earth is without sin and its consequences. This is the fulfilment of Christ taking away the sin of the world. All is perfect and in no way tedious, because our life and imaginations are totally free without the sin in our hearts dragging us down. Total freedom. We live, invent, explore, create and love in fellowship and to the glory of God who we now know intimately.

To illustrate this, God uses the picture of marriage. The intimate relationship between a husband and wife is the closest love relationship we have on this earth. Scripture tells us it is a picture of our spiritual eternal relationship with Christ. The believers in Jesus, referred to as the 'Church' in Scripture and, in the future, as the 'new

Jerusalem', are also spoken of as the wife of the Lamb, who is Christ:

> 'Let us be glad and rejoice and give Him glory, for the marriage of the Lamb has come, and His wife has made herself ready.' And to her it was granted to be arrayed in fine linen, clean and bright, for the fine linen is the righteous acts of the saints (Revelation 19:7–8).

'Saints' in Scripture simply refers to everyone who believes. We are described as 'righteous' because of Christ's death:

> For He made Him who knew no sin to be sin for us, that we might become the righteousness of God in Him (2 Corinthians 5:21).

> For by one offering He has perfected forever those who are being sanctified (Hebrews 10:14).

'Sanctified' is the word used to describe the work of the Holy Spirit, making us more like Christ. When he is at work in us, every act of obedience to him is described as a 'righteous act'. The people in heaven are not presented as mere spectators of God's glory. They are participants in his glory, they themselves 'having the glory of God' (Revelation 21:11). And the most amazing thing is that God is not simply 'putting up with us'.

He delights in us as his new creations, and lives in the midst of us.

I have stayed on a number of occasions in the south of England at a boarding school situated close to a village. I have often smiled when recalling the story of how the school came to be situated so idyllically. It used to be a grand house for a family of the aristocracy. They liked their house, but the view of the peasants in the village spoilt it for them. Instead of moving themselves, they moved the entire village and its houses, so they were out of their sight. I know of other examples of this in rural England.

It is not surprising, because that is how our world is. The powerful, influential and moneyed people choose to live separately from poor people. Even today there are clubs, places of entertainment, restaurants and the likes which are exclusively for the rich and powerful to enable them to avoid the 'common people'.

Jesus himself commented a number of times on this characteristic of our world. On one occasion when his disciples were arguing about who should be the greatest among them, he said:

> The kings of the Gentiles exercise lordship over them, and those who exercise authority over them are called 'benefactors'. But not so among you; on the contrary, he who is greatest among you, let him

> be as the younger, and he who governs as he who serves. For who is greater, he who sits at the table, or he who serves? Is it not he who sits at the table? Yet I am among you as the One who serves' (Luke 22:25–27).

In this world, the rich and powerful are content with their title of 'benefactor'. They are happy to live separately in luxury while advising, and contributing, here and there as they choose. How different Jesus was when he came to this earth. He was here to serve. And how different heaven is. God is for us; more than that he loves us; more than that he chooses not to live detached from us and have an occasional visit but to live in our midst. Jesus really is the image of God, isn't he?

God desires to live in our midst because, in his sight, we are already 'justified' and acceptable. We have been since the moment we believed, but on the new earth we will have been perfected. We are described as coming to the 'church of the firstborn who are registered in heaven, to God the Judge of all, to the spirits of just men made perfect' (Hebrews 12:23).

Jesus' teaching on heaven opens and expands our minds to see this life as very brief, in comparison to life in eternity. It is like installing a roof window in our souls. We can now see heavenwards. And we begin to see how significant Christ's death and resurrection really are. It is the turning point for the whole cosmos.

We read in Scripture that when human beings first rebelled against God it affected the whole of creation. The apostle Paul personifies the created world to explain the present situation:

> The creation itself also will be delivered from the bondage of corruption into the glorious liberty of the children of God. For we know that the whole creation groans and labours with birth pangs together until now. Not only that, but we also who have the firstfruits of the Spirit, even we ourselves groan within ourselves, eagerly waiting for the adoption, the redemption of our body (Romans 8:21–23).

The present world we live in anticipates being renewed into a new earth, in the same way believers in Christ look forward to 'the redemption of our body'.

Paul is saying that the present world we live in anticipates being renewed into a new earth, in the same way believers in Christ look forward to 'the redemption of our body'. Paul explains, in his letter to the church at Corinth, the hope and expectation of every believer in Christ for the future:

> The dead will be raised incorruptible, and we

> shall be changed.... Then shall be brought to pass the saying that is written: 'Death is swallowed up in victory' (1 Corinthians 15:52, 54).

A new earth, and us with new resurrected bodies in the likeness of Christ's resurrection body, with God living in our midst. This is our hope. Is it delusional? Listen to what Paul says: 'For we were saved in this hope, but hope that is seen is not hope; for why does one still hope for what he sees?' (Romans 8:24). God, we remember, does not lie. When someone believes what God has said because they trust him, they see his future promises as reality.

Some of my greatest joys on this earth have come when I have witnessed such confidence:

- When Dorothy heard of the unexpected death of her beloved husband, from a rookie policeman who trembled when he brought her the news, she was able to sit him down and make him a cup of tea, calming him by explaining to him God was in control.
- When Michael was visited by the local policeman to tell him his young daughter had been killed in a car crash, he responded by quoting something Job said in the Old Testament:

  > The Lord gave, and the Lord has taken away; blessed be the name of the Lord (Job 1:21).

> The now retired policeman tells the story to this day because it had such an effect on him.

Both Dorothy and Michael were two of the most intelligent people I have ever known. I add that simply because I have heard the lie so often that it is only uneducated, ignorant people who would believe such a thing.

Not all believers can however confront death with such confidence. Temptations can often come along with the severest of trials, and our hope is always in Christ and not the quantity or quality of our faith. Nevertheless, many are able to follow Paul's example when he says:

> For to me, to live is Christ, and to die is gain. But if I live on in the flesh, this will mean fruit from my labour; yet what I shall choose I cannot tell. For I am hard-pressed between the two, having a desire to depart and be with Christ, which is far better (Philippians 1:21–23).

It is not that Christians are longing to die. They understand their life is full of purpose and God is in control. But they also understand that 'what you sow is not made alive unless it dies' (1 Corinthians 15:36). Death is the exit from this world but the entrance to life everlasting.

I have, perhaps like you, been to a number of funerals. This message of heaven is often brought as reassurance to those present, with no reference to whether the deceased believed in Christ or not. It is, I think, one of the most cowardly of lies, to pretend Jesus said everyone will go to heaven. If someone believes everyone will go to heaven, then that is their view. But to stand as a representative of Jesus at a funeral and say Jesus said everyone goes to heaven is simply a lie.

This is what he said:

> Most assuredly, I say to you, he who hears My word and believes in Him who sent Me has everlasting life, and shall not come into judgement, but has passed from death into life.
>
> Most assuredly, I say to you, the hour is coming, and now is, when the dead will hear the voice of the Son of God; and those who hear will live. For as the Father has life in Himself, so He has granted the Son to have life in Himself, and has given Him authority to execute judgement also, because He is the Son of Man. Do not marvel at this; for the hour is coming in which all who are in the graves will hear His voice and come forth—those who have done good, to the resurrection of life, and those who have done evil, to the resurrection of condemnation (John 5:24–29).

What do you think? This is clearly not merely the teaching of someone who is attempting to add his own insights to the wisdom of this world. Is he deluded or mad? Is he a liar? Or is he exactly who he says he is?

He is saying God's great plan of saving grace comes to its completion in the new heavens and earth. We are changed here in this rebellious world, but then is the completion.

I have heard on numerous occasions people say, 'If God is really in control, why doesn't he do something!' The answer according to Scripture is that he has done something. Not only has he sent his Son to save all who believe in him, but the continuing existence of this world in its present form is to give time for people to repent so they do not perish. The world remains as it is because of God's love and mercy, 'that all should come to repentance' (2 Peter 3:9).

But the time is limited. Please do not wait until you die; that will be too late. Eventually our world will burn up. But then, after the judgement, comes a new world—a world of perfection, when all will see God really did do something.

If we believe Christ now, we will experience 'grace upon grace', culminating in eternal life in heaven. That is the promise of Jesus Christ.

8 Jesus 'declares' God

The Gospel of John, chapter 1, verse 18 says:

No one has seen God at any time. The only begotten Son, who is in the bosom of the Father, He has declared Him.

We come now to the last verse of what is often described as John's prologue. These first eighteen verses serve as a grand entrance hall to the rest of the Gospel. Imagine a stately home which contains art and treasures of all kinds. We walk through the main door and are transported into what seems a different world to what we are accustomed. The magnificence of all we see at first glance causes us to take our time and look at each item carefully. We work our way slowly round the hall:

- We see a description of Jesus.
- We hear a commentary given by the very best, qualified man to explain what Jesus was doing.
- We, then, hear a critical assessment of what is on display: those for and those against.
- As we work our way round the room, we learn of the great benefits Jesus brings from his best friend—the man in charge of the gallery.
- As we complete our circular tour of the entrance hall, we are told what those benefits mean to us.

We now know what this exhibition is about and, if we choose to continue through this great mansion, we will see the themes from the entrance hall revisited and explained fully.

I hope you want to read through the rest of John's Gospel. But we have not quite yet finished with the entrance hall. As we approach the place we first entered, we come to our last verse. By design, it is a return to the theme begun in our opening verse.

How, we ask, can anyone genuinely know anything about God? After all, 'No one has seen God at any time.' We read in Scripture that God is a Spirit and is therefore invisible to us. We often have God revealed to us in terms of having eyes, ears, arms and so on, but it is generally understood that this is God explaining himself in ways we can understand and to which we can relate. The reality is, he is invisible, so no one has ever seen him.

Yet here is a presentation of Jesus Christ, who is the Word, the Lamb of God, the Saviour, the Messiah, the Son of Man, Immanuel, the Way the Truth and the Life, and here in verse 18, 'the only begotten Son' of God. You could perhaps multiply these names by ten for a complete set given to us in Scripture. These are, however, enough for us to know he 'is in the bosom of the Father'.

This phrase, 'in the bosom of the Father', may sound a quaint expression to us, but it is ideal in reflecting the intimacy and love between the Father and the Son. The

Lord Jesus Christ knows the Father to such an extent we can be confident that all he reveals is a mirror image of who God is and what he is like.

John, here, echoes what he told us in his opening verse. He presents Jesus as the Word and the Son who is with God and yet, at the same time, is God. When he was here on earth, he was subservient to his Father, while remaining equal with him.

The Scriptures are clear when presenting who God is; there is a consistency and unity. They tell us there is only one God. They, then, unfold the teaching that the Father is fully God; Jesus, his Son, is fully God; and the Holy Spirit is fully God—yet only one God. It is not difficult to understand what the Bible is actually saying. The difficulty is in the whole concept of a God who is three in one.

Many illustrations have been given to try and explain how this can be, but all the ones I have seen only manage to give a false picture of what Scripture says. Perhaps there is no illustration possible because there is nothing we can liken his plurality to in our experience. This should not surprise us. Even understanding one single human being fully is out of our range. How much more so with God himself? How can a damaged,

How can a damaged, finite mind, ever truly comprehend the greatness of an infinite God?

finite mind, ever truly comprehend the greatness of an infinite God?

Yet even though we cannot fully understand him, we can know him. We are glad God does not demand from us a full understanding of who he is, but he does require us to trust him. When considering God's infinite greatness, we have to confess that we know very little, and what we do know is down to God's extraordinary kindness in bringing the revelation of himself to us in a way we can understand.

But we can know something of God because 'The only begotten Son, who is in the bosom of the Father, He has declared Him.' Christ is openly and emphatically making a formal announcement concerning God. We do not have to guess any more.

This declaration of God includes showing us why God has chosen to make himself known. He continues to create, and even now his purpose is to make a new universe which is without sin. It is not as if he is just beginning this work. The greatest historical event this world has known or will know is the death and resurrection of Jesus. It was there that the foundation of a new universe was laid when he dealt once and for all with the sin problem.

One of the things Jesus said when he hung on the cross was, 'It is finished!' (John 19:30). We have noted already that the reason he came to this world was 'to save sinners' (1 Timothy 1:15). That was his assignment. As far as Jesus was concerned his assignment had been accomplished.

He had not merely tried to save sinners, nor had he simply made it possible for them to be saved. He had come to save them and that is what he did.

We live on the edge of moorland where sheep graze. It is not uncommon during the winter months for snow to drift and be a danger to the sheep. Imagine a situation where it has been snowing heavily, and the shepherd is concerned that the sheep on the higher levels are in danger. He says to his son:

'Go up to the top field and rescue those sheep. Bring them down here and put them in the barn for the night.'

His lad puts on his waterproofs and trudges up the hill to the sheep. Through deepening snow, he finally arrives at the top field. With a great deal of effort, he opens the gate and provides a way of escape for the sheep to get down to lower ground. He, then, makes his way back to the farmhouse and opens the barn door, wedging the doors open with a couple of bricks.

When he was back in the farmhouse, removing his waterproofs and boots, his father asks, 'Did you rescue them? Are they safe in the barn?'

'Well,' says the son, 'I opened the top gate for them, and if they have any sense, they can make their way down here. I've left the barn door open for them.'

I think his father would not be over pleased—mission still unaccomplished. The son could not say, 'Job done; it is finished'.

I am guessing the father would send his son back up to the top field to bring them down to safety.

This is not what happened when the Father sent his Son to save his sheep. Jesus is often described as a Shepherd in Scripture and, those who believe in him as the sheep. John, later on in his Gospel records Jesus as saying:

> 'I am the good shepherd; and I know My sheep, and am known by My own. As the Father knows Me, even so I know the Father; and I lay down My life for the sheep' (John 10:14–15).

He goes on to say:

> 'My sheep hear My voice, and I know them, and they follow Me. And I give them eternal life, and they shall never perish; neither shall anyone snatch them out of My hand. My Father, who has given them to Me, is greater than all' (John 10:27–29).

The death of Jesus, then, is the central pivot in God's plans for a new creation. Christ did what he came to do: deal with sin and save sinners. Christ not only shows us the characteristics of his Father but, practically and in real time, demonstrates the love God has for us by dying for his sheep. He came to save them, and that is what he did.

HOW DO WE RESPOND TO JESUS' DECLARATION OF GOD THE FATHER?

After accomplishing the central necessity by Christ's

death, we now live in the phase of God's plan where he is gathering together those who will inhabit the new earth he is creating.

Jesus gives us a parable of a man who organized a banquet and sent out his invitations. One after the other they gave their apologies for not being able to attend because they were too busy with other concerns. We read:

> Then the master of the house, being angry, said to his servant, 'Go out quickly into the streets and lanes of the city, and bring in here the poor and the maimed and the lame and the blind.' And the servant said, 'Master, it is done as you commanded, and still there is room.' Then the master said to the servant, 'Go out into the highways and hedges, and compel them to come in, that my house may be filled' (Luke 14:21–23).

We have a picture of heaven given to us when John says:

> After these things I looked, and behold, a great multitude which no one could number, of all nations, tribes, peoples, and tongues, standing before the throne and before the Lamb, clothed with white robes, with palm branches in their hands, and crying out with a loud voice, saying, 'Salvation belongs to our God who sits on the throne, and to the Lamb!' (Revelation 7:9–10).

Jesus, in his parable, was making the point that heaven will not be only for a few, but for multitudes.

Throughout the Bible, we have numerous invitations given to us from God to come to him: 'Look to Me, and be saved, all you ends of the earth!' (Isaiah 45:22). This example makes clear the invitation is for all people everywhere, including you and me. John, in his Gospel, records one of Jesus' invitations to us: 'If anyone thirsts, let him come to Me and drink. He who believes in Me, as the Scripture has said, out of his heart will flow rivers of living water.' But this He spoke concerning the Spirit, whom those believing in Him would receive (John 7:37–39).

In all the tumult and noise of our world, with all the differing world views vying for attention, there is one Shepherd's voice calling out for his sheep.

This is where the history of our world stands. God is inviting us to himself. Even if many do not accept his invitation, this is not a futile exercise, because we have heard Jesus say: 'My sheep hear My voice, and I know them, and they follow Me.'

In all the tumult and noise of our world, with all the differing world views vying for attention, there is one Shepherd's voice calling out for his sheep. That voice is ignored by all except those who recognize his voice. They see him, not as a madman, nor a liar and deceiver, but as the authentic Son of God. They alter their course, turn around in repentance, and place their faith in him to follow.

I pray this may be true of you.

The Gospel writer, John, also wrote three letters we can read in the Bible. He tells us the reason he wrote his first letter in his closing comments:

> God has given us eternal life, and this life is in His Son. He who has the Son has life; he who does not have the Son of God does not have life. These things I have written to you who believe in the name of the Son of God, that you may know that you have eternal life, and that you may continue to believe in the name of the Son of God (1 John 5:11–13).

Believers, says John, can know they have eternal life. It is not so impossible after all. It is certainly *incredible*, ***but definitely not*** *uncredible.*

Believers, says John, can know they have eternal life. It is not so impossible after all. It is certainly *incredible*, but definitely not *uncredible*. The phrase, 'He who has the Son has life,' is simply speaking of those who believe in Jesus, and the life spoken of is eternal.

The characteristics John gives in this letter to identify true believers in Jesus are threefold:

- Those who recognize who Jesus is. They can identify who Jesus is and believe in his name.
- They turn from their sin to live a life in obedience to him.
- They love one another.

It is because of this last characteristic that believers can be found meeting together in fellowship to worship God together. If you believe in the Lord Jesus Christ, do not imagine it is a private decision you keep to yourself. Once converted, we now identify with other believers who we recognize as our brothers and sisters; we are baptized in the name of Christ and grow together as we hear the Bible explained on a regular basis.

This is what is happening today all over the world. The reason being, the Church belongs to Christ, and he is the head of it. His promise is, 'I will build My church, and the gates of Hades shall not prevail against it' (Matthew 16:18).

Often, people use the word, 'church', when referring to a building used for Christian worship. In Scripture, however, it is always used to describe the assembly of believers. It is a reference to people, not buildings. The Church did not originally have buildings of their own. We can now know what Paul was saying when he described the Church as 'the pillar and ground of the truth' (1 Timothy 3:15). As Jesus has declared God to us, so those who believe in him have the task together of upholding him and his message as true. We are told 'to contend earnestly for the faith which was once for all delivered to the saints' (Jude 1:3). The message of the gospel has been entrusted to believers. It is interesting to note that it was not given to high-ranking individuals or any organization. It is, therefore, the responsibility of all Christians to ensure the gospel message is passed on faithfully to the next generation.

When someone believes in Christ, they are not looking for a building to attend to express their faith, they are looking for fellow believers so they may join them in their declaration of God and his gospel. Depending on where you live, those who believe in Christ may meet in a building which has been specifically built for that purpose, or they may not. It is to the people who believe that a new Christian is drawn, so they may worship, grow and serve in what is described as the body of Christ. Referring to the Church, the apostle Paul tells us, 'Now you are the body of Christ, and members individually' (1 Corinthians 12–27).

If you desire to follow Christ, be careful not to make the same mistake as me when I first became a Christian. I presumed a building referred to as a 'church' would guarantee that believers in Christ could be found there. It wasn't the case for me. The Bible was read, but never explained, and it didn't take long to find out why. It was because they didn't believe it was true. As a result of that, they did not know who Jesus is nor his message, let alone proclaim it. But they did like being religious. Take care!

We respond to Christ's declaration of his Father, by hearing his voice and following him. We have seen this involves faith, repentance, and confessing Christ openly by being baptized. We identify ourselves with other believers to take an active role as members of Christ's body.

This phase of God's plan continues, but only until Christ returns. The gospel message is urgent.

In Matthew 24, he tells us we are to observe what is happening in our world and recognize the signs which indicate all is now ready for his return. Read through them and see if you agree with me that we cannot be complacent. The day and hour of his return has already been set. But Jesus warns us:

> 'But of that day and hour no one knows, not even the angels of heaven, but My Father only ... Therefore, you also be ready, for the Son of Man is coming at an hour you do not expect' (Matthew 24:36, 44).

We can look forward with hope and expectation to the glorious future God is preparing for those who love him.

When we consider the priorities in our lives, what could possibly be more important than being ready for that time when we come face to face with God? All we need is a simple, childlike trust in

Jesus Christ. There is, then, no need to fear the future or Christ's return. Instead, we can look forward with hope and expectation to the glorious future God is preparing for those who love him.